$1.50

[T]he Poet in the Poem

The Personae of Eliot, Yeats, and Pound

BY GEORGE T. WRIGHT

UNIVERSITY OF CALIFORNIA PRESS

FORSYTH LIBRARY - FHSU

THE POET IN THE POEM

Furnished by Publisher
as Perspectives in Criticism, 4.

George T. Wright

The Poet in the Poem

THE PERSONAE OF ELIOT, YEATS, AND POUND

UNIVERSITY OF CALIFORNIA PRESS
Berkeley and Los Angeles
1962

Second printing, 1962
(First Paper-bound Edition)

University of California Press
Berkeley and Los Angeles, California
Cambridge University Press
London, England

LIBRARY OF CONGRESS CATALOG CARD NUMBER: 59-14483
Printed in the United States of America

To Jerry

—FOR LISTENING AND, YES, FOR TALKING

Preface

ONE OF THE WORDS frequently heard in discussions of modern poetry is "impersonality." Poets in general, but especially those poets we think of as difficult—Eliot, Pound, Yeats, Stevens, and their many *semblables* and *frères*—are acknowledged by most critics to have converted poetry from a personal communication into an impersonal creation. The modern poem is often cold and hard, according to the prescription of T. E. Hulme; not warm and intimate in the manner of most nineteenth-century verse. To be sure, many poets still writing today compose works that seem no less personal than those of Wordsworth and Keats. But the most influential and prominent poets of the early twentieth century have gone another way, into what we call, without too well knowing what it is, impersonality.

Perhaps the extreme of impersonality is reached in the poetry of Wallace Stevens. "Peter Quince at the Clavier," for example, is a series of exquisitely modeled tableaux in which the feelings of Susanna and the elders are successively immobilized in a sort of verbal sculpture, and the ancient story serves to illustrate the nature of music. The people are of an importance subordinate to that of their gestures and to that of the color, the tone, the "idea" of their action; and the action in turn enforces the generalization about *human* feeling, not merely the feeling of the poet, which the poem expounds.

Gorgeously stylized as they are, however, the human figures in this poem are exceptional in Stevens' poetry; his poems usually contain no people at all, or present the merest human shadows who function mostly as types and for the location of a thought or for its abstract embodiment in the form of a trope. That the ideas that Stevens is at pains to formulate have mainly to do with patterns and systems of human feeling cannot make us forget how few in this poetry are the people who feel. In spite of the many images that make vivid his cold and abstract propositions, in spite even of the urgency of the rhythms, the absence of people makes us feel the impersonality of the work. Even the poet himself is absent: only a very few poems—notably "Farewell to Florida" and "Loneliness in Jersey City"—can be said to deal with a self that specifically belongs to Wallace Stevens. The comments on human nature almost always appear in abstract form:

> Two things of opposite natures seem to depend
> On one another, as a man depends
> On a woman, day on night, the imagined
>
> On the real. This is the origin of change.

And even the climax, effective as it is, mutes its human relevance:

> Winter and spring, cold copulars, embrace
> And forth the particulars of rapture come.
> [*CPWS*, 392]

The verse has the warmth attendant on rich imagery and rich versification, yet seems still coldly human. In Stevens' last two volumes, *The Auroras of Autumn* and *The Rock*, even the abstract "I" tends to disappear. First person singular personal pronouns occur only thirty-five times, and all but one of these refer to a character, usually dim, whom Stevens represents as talking, not to Stevens himself. Only once in a hundred and twenty-one pages does the poet use any form of this pronoun to refer to his otherwise totally unobtrusive self.

And yet for all its impersonality Stevens' poetry is entirely individual. Like other contemporary poets, he cultivates a style that we cannot mistake for any other writer's. His verse, like that of Yeats, Eliot, Pound, Marianne Moore, Auden, Dylan Thomas, and many other modern poets, is easy to recognize because of its many individual characteristics. And the same critics who speak of impersonality continually apprise us of the existence of "new voices" in poetry, of poets whose ways of looking at life are "peculiarly their own." For an impersonal art this poetry seems to be surprisingly personal, or at least curiously individual.

Our main difficulty in disposing of these apparent contradictions seems to be our confusion over what we mean by "personal poetry," and we cannot clarify this term until we understand something about the various ways in which a poet is present in his poems. The very existence of the problem is obscured by all the nineteenth-century poetry that tends to regard as more or less identical the several faces of the poet which appear both in and out of the poem. The frequent necessity of making a distinction between the poet and his personae —that is, the characters who speak the words of the poems—has lately become a critical commonplace. But that every poem contains such a persona, and that other versions of the poet exist within the poem, are truths that, as they require argument, also promise illumination.

The main aims of this study, then, are to gain some understanding of the ways in which poets are present in their poems in any age, and to use that understanding to discover in what senses such modern poetry as that of Eliot, Yeats, and Pound can be called impersonal. Since the modern poets examined are only three, the practices common to all of them may at most be inferred to be common to other poets of their school, but not necessarily to modern poets of different persuasions. At the same time, in the light of the analysis of the various faces of the poet, it will be possible to make a small number of generalizations about modern poetry as well as about poetry of any age.

But in addition to the aim of throwing light on the work of Eliot, Yeats, and Pound, this study aims to serve as an introduction to the study of personae and of the place of the poet in his poem. The closer one looks at poetic speakers, the more immense the subject seems; though the persona appears to be a fairly simple poetic element, it quickly leads the student deep into the structural bases of poetry. And as the great area it opens up has for so long remained virtually unexamined, I have limited my own explorations to the part of it that seems central and thus relevant to the modest and immediate purposes of this study. The resultant sketch does no more than suggest what a painstaking scholarly analysis of personae in literature might reveal about the nature of the art.

For permission to quote copyrighted materials I am indebted to several persons and publishers. I am grateful to Mr. Richard Eberhart and the Oxford University Press for permission to quote from "The Groundhog"; to Mr. Robert Mayo and the Department of English of Northwestern University for permission to quote from the *Analyst;* and to Mr. Ezra Pound and his literary agent in the United Kingdom, Mr. Arthur V. Moore, for permission to quote from several of Pound's works. The following publishers have also permitted me to quote from these works: Methuen & Co., Ltd., from T. S. Eliot's *The Sacred Wood;* Rupert Hart-Davis Limited, and the Macmillan Company, from *The Letters of W. B. Yeats,* edited by Allan Wade; the Macmillan Company, Mrs. W. B. Yeats, and A. P. Watt & Son, from Yeats's *Collected Poems, Autobiography, A Vision,* and *The Cut-*

ting of an Agate. Harcourt, Brace and Company, Inc., who hold the copyrights to *The Letters of Ezra Pound 1907–1941,* edited by D. D. Paige, copyright 1950; to *Selected Essays, 1917–1932* by T. S. Eliot, copyright 1932; and to *Collected Poems 1909–1935* by T. S. Eliot, copyright 1936, have permitted me to quote from these works and from *Four Quartets* by T. S. Eliot, copyright 1943 by T. S. Eliot. They have also permitted me to reprint Richard Wilbur's poem, "Praise in Summer," from *The Beautiful Changes And Other Poems,* copyright 1947 by Richard Wilbur; and Faber and Faber, Ltd., holders of the British rights, have permitted me to quote the same poem from Wilbur's *Poems 1943–56.* I am also permitted to quote from *An Examination of Ezra Pound,* edited by Peter Russell, copyright 1950, all rights reserved, reprinted by permission of New Directions; and from these works by Ezra Pound: *Guide to Kulchur,* copyright 1938, all rights reserved, reprinted by permission of New Directions; *Literary Essays of Ezra Pound,* edited and introduced by T. S. Eliot, copyright 1954, all rights reserved, reprinted by permission of New Directions; *Personae: Collected Shorter Poems of Ezra Pound,* copyright 1926, 1954 by Ezra Pound, reprinted by permission of New Directions; and *The Cantos of Ezra Pound,* copyright 1934, 1937, 1940, 1948 by Ezra Pound, reprinted by permission of New Directions.

Beyond the courtesies acknowledged above, several persons have contributed substantially and in various ways to the reduction of the shortcomings of this book. In its early stages Professors Thomas F. Parkinson and Warren Ramsey offered me friendly encouragement as well as scholarly assistance. The Editorial Committee and Mr. Glenn Gosling, both of the University of California Press, have placed me in their debt for their wise advice and for their kindness in giving it. What I, along with so many others, owe to the warmth and intelligence of Josephine Miles, neither this note nor this book can adequately suggest. Finally, although the dedication implies in part how greatly my wife has helped me both with ideas and with details, my gratitude for her wit and for her love wants to be set down again here.

G. T. W.

Contents

Titles of Abbreviated Sources

ELIOT

CPP — *Complete Poems and Plays, 1909–1950.* New York: Harcourt, Brace, 1952.

SE — *Selected Essays, 1917–1932.* New ed. New York: Harcourt, Brace, 1950.

SW — *The Sacred Wood.* London: Methuen, 1948.

YEATS

Auto — *The Autobiography of William Butler Yeats.* New York: Macmillan, 1953.

CA — *The Cutting of an Agate.* New York: Macmillan, 1912.

CP — *The Collected Poems of W. B. Yeats.* New York: Macmillan, 1956.

Letters — *The Letters of W. B. Yeats,* ed. Allan Wade. New York: Macmillan, 1954.

Vision — *A Vision.* New York: Macmillan, 1956.

POUND

GB — *Gaudier-Brzeska: A Memoir by Ezra Pound.* London: The Bodley Head, 1916.

GK — *Guide to Kulchur.* Norfolk, Conn.: New Directions, 1952.

Inst — *Instigations of Ezra Pound.* New York: Boni and Liveright, 1920.

LE — *Literary Essays of Ezra Pound,* ed. with introd. T. S. Eliot. London: Faber and Faber, 1954.

Letters — *The Letters of Ezra Pound 1907–1941,* ed. D. D. Paige. New York: Harcourt, Brace, 1950.

SR — *The Spirit of Romance.* London: Peter Owen, 1952.

OTHERS

CPWS — *The Collected Poems of Wallace Stevens.* New York: Alfred A. Knopf, 1954.

Essays — Oscar Wilde. *Essays.* London: Methuen, 1950.

1

The Faces of the Poet

THE PROBLEM OF personae is closely related to the problem of the nature of human personality. In one sense, surely, people are what they appear; in one sense, too, the poet is what he seems to be in his poems. In both instances the person *is* what he *does;* his actions define him. But as soon as we begin to interpret those actions, we begin to lose our objectivity in observing him. A man says "Oh!" or commits a murder. If we merely observe these facts, we can state them without severe distortion; but we usually feel that mere objective statement is inaccurate, that the lack of distortion is itself distortion because the fact is, if not misinterpreted, also not *fully* described. We want to locate the word or the action in a universe of words and actions, to relate it intelligibly to other data we have observed and to other interpretations (possibly mistaken and certainly incomplete) that we have made. In order to understand anything at all about a person, we must develop a view of his conduct as a whole and relate our interpretation of him to our interpretation of other people and other things. Sometimes we formulate these views in words, and sometimes we merely assume them, unspoken, as the never articulated but continually revised bases of all our own relevant actions.

Persons, poems, and ideas have similar effects on our grasp of things: all of them alter in some way the structure of the universe which we have previously accepted. Every action, every day, every year, makes more complex our view of the world we live in. Life is full of surprises and constantly demands that we revise —practically if not verbally, and in detail if not in design—our conceptions of the world, and hence our attitudes toward it, and hence our actions in it. Thus behind every word we utter, behind every gesture we make, lies a world of cerebration incalculably complex, and what we are, though it is theoretically readable in what we do, is only partially knowable, by ourselves or by others, without a total knowledge of our nervous systems and all their records. Since no science and no technology can ever reveal such information to anyone, full objective knowledge of any person is unattainable. We have always to be content with interpretations based on what are really very few pieces of evidence. Even the subtlest student of his own mind, however intricate his sense of himself, knows how little information he possesses on the subject of which he knows most.

But human beings do not require full information before they evaluate what information they have. Even if we know how extraordinarily complex all persons are, we evaluate them, in one way or another, at every meeting. At every point in our experience with a person we entertain a general picture, an impression, of his reality, an impression that yields in turn, as we discover more both about our world and about him, to clearer and fuller impressions. Few persons will ever substantially affect our general view of the world; as we meet them, as we understand them better, we fit them in, making them accord with, without much expanding, our knowledge of what is what. At every level of society various popular or esoteric formulations help us in this process of assimilation: sociological, biological, anthropological, historical or cultural notions provide us with rough formulas for the evaluation of the people we meet. Our past experience, deeply structured, offers us techniques for reworking present materials into new structures.

But no view of the world is really large enough to comprehend all that is in the world. Not to exclude is not to interpret; not to interpret is not to be humanly conscious. People with values extremely different from ours we tend to think of as stupid or vicious or insane; what we really mean is that their words and actions are beyond the capacity of our nervous or social structures to assimilate. For a view of the world involves also a system of expectations: we expect our future to be rather like our past, we expect history to repeat itself, we expect the people, the ideas, even the poems, we meet to be not notably dissimilar to those with which we are already acquainted. Confronted with experience totally unlike that we know, we find that our view of life will not "give" so much as to admit it. Like some medieval and some nonmedieval thinkers, we refuse to accord to the unassimilable the honor of existence, or we label it as morally or mentally insane—which is only to say that for us it has no place in the universe.

The system of expectations which accompanies a view of life is flexible enough to admit minor variations on familiar experiences but not to accept extreme surprises. Single such surprises will probably be discounted, but if they repeatedly occur, a person must either evolve a broader view of the conditions of human life or give way under the conflict between what he expects there to be and what is. Certainly to a large extent cultures and persons refuse to recognize what they find incompatible with their preferred interpretations of reality; perhaps nothing in human history has caused so much trouble as the failure of groups of people to acknowledge, or even to see, not the truth of their opponents' beliefs so much as the palpable insufficiency of their own. At the same time, the nervous systems of some individuals seem to develop a high degree of tolerance for at least certain kinds of newnesses; many persons—innovators in various fields, for example, or some of the insane—learn to live with situations that most human beings who share their cultural backgrounds would regard as insupportable.

In most of us there is a constant battle between the schematizations of reality which we set up for ourselves and the life that, as we meet it, continually exceeds the bounds of those schematizations. We learn. Our expectations are repeatedly surprised, and we meet the shock by gradually evolving somewhat more inclusive schematizations: we recognize another kind of person, or we slightly revise our view of the world as we see the implications of a new idea. Or, on the other hand, we forget: we close up certain portions of our minds as the experiences we meet no longer seem to require their use. Poems meet our expectations or surprise us just as persons and ideas do. We accept or reject them according to how they fit into our views of what is, and therefore of what should be, poetry. We even react so to the elements of poems—to the images, to the figures, to the plot, to the characters. We expect them all to be variations of what we have met before. While we may embrace novelty, we embrace it only within certain limits —in poetry as in life.

And so with personae. Poems, we think, may be spoken by any kind of character. Within limits it is so, but the limits exist, and they narrow the range from which a poet may choose his speakers. Swift's personae will not do for Shelley; Shelley's would not have done for Chaucer; Chaucer's are unsuitable for Eliot. This is partly because of differences between the poets, partly because of differences between the eras, partly because of differences in the genres preferred by each writer. But the poet's choice of personae always reflects the reader's sense of what is permissible, and the reader's sense of this is based on his past experience of personae and of the works of art in which they appear.

But personae are like persons in another way, too. Because we expect certain conduct from them, they conform to our expectations. People develop likes, dislikes, convictions, habits, hobbies, styles, attitudes, which are intelligible only in the context of the culture in which they live. Everyone assumes certain roles, which alter slightly as he moves from one situation to another or from one group to another. Our audience largely determines the face we shall put on; but even in solitude we attitudinize according to the attitudinizing conventions of our age. We are, even to ourselves as far as we can see, intelligible only in the terms our age uses to describe and understand people. To adopt roles too far removed from the conventional roles of our time is to be, in our time, insane.

Thus a poet's personae are limited on two sides—first, by the expectations of his audience, and, second, by his own choice, narrowed by those expectations, of one or more culturally possible roles. The process is inevitably confusing. We pretend in life to meet individual persons, yet we greet them largely as types; though each of us is a distinct person, we create for ourselves roles. So the reader of literature expects to meet people—personae and poets—whom he can in effect, if not in words, formulate, whom he can fit into his scheme of things; and so the poet, too, assumes in any poem roles that his reader will "understand."

As we pursue our reading of any poem, therefore, we acquire a fuller impression both of the persona and of the poet, and we accord our pictures of them with what our experience of other poems has led us to expect of personae and poets. These expectations are never simple. They vary, surely, from reader to reader because no one's sense of literature is quite identical with anyone else's. They vary even more widely from age to age as new ideas both of poetic and nonpoetic phenomena effect changes in cultural attitudes. But so long as art is art, our expectations must have some common basis superior to all variation. The poem, to every reader in every age, must be a poem; and because a poem is speech, there must exist a speaker, a persona, to say the words.

II

The term, persona, drawn as it is from drama, involves the image of a speaking man even when, as in recent centuries, the voice of the speaker of nondramatic verse has ceased to be a voice—or, at least, when the speaker is heard without ever having spoken. Though we recognize the differences between writing and speech, we nevertheless apply to writing many terms that are borrowed from our criticism of speech: tone, intonation, pitch, accent, voice, to mention only a few. And we pretend that poetry on a page has sound in the way that something spoken has sound. Nevertheless, the way in which writing is speech, the way in which it is sound, are peculiar. We read into every poem the sounds that we hear, the voice that we assume—as, to be sure, the writer expects us to do. His writing is based on the expectation that we will do so, and on the further expectation that behind every group of words we will sense not only sounds and a voice but a person. For every composer of a literary work of art knows, whether he recognizes his knowledge or not, that words are always spoken in what we call the first person, that words, whatever their value in expressing objective facts, always represent someone talking.

Just as language itself sets up limits within which dialogues may take place—as two persons, for example, expect each other to converse in a language intelligible to both and not in a foreign language, and expect each other to use a limited range of diction, sentence structure, and other speech elements—so literature is limited to certain areas of speech considered appropriate by readers and writers alike. The principle of decorum operates not only to confine the artist of an age and country to the language of his age and country; it confines him also to what we call the language of literature. He must observe not only the conventions of contemporary utterance and the conventions of contemporary artistic utterance; he must observe also the conventions of *all* artistic utterance. His poems must be poems, and the speakers of his poems—his personae—must bear to the poem and to the poet certain relationships that prevail throughout all literary works.

As soon as we recognize that in all poems it is a persona, not a poet, who speaks the actual words, we can see the fundamental dramatic character even of lyric verse. In noting this character we seem almost to be effecting an identity between two opposite poles of literary production. For although every speaker in a play is, for the duration of his speech, a lyric self, a presenter of a point of view, dramatic form requires that one speaker's person be confronted with another. In their "pure" forms the lyric presents one speaker, the drama more than one. We call lyrical, therefore, those dramas in which one character (with his point of view) so predominates that his confrontations of other characters seem falsified: the meetings with other personae are merely opportunities for their spiritual domination by the hero.

Similarly, the lyric is or becomes dramatic when it presents not a single point of view but a struggle between conflicting points of view. The deliberate placing of a distance between the poet and his lyric persona effectively dramatizes the substance of the poem. But, however accustomed we may be to the more direct lyric in which the thoughts or feelings of the poet, or of the characters he represents, are stated with unambiguous explicitness, art is formal, and there must always be a distance, minimized or emphasized, between the maker of the poem and the persons in the poem. Poetry, dramatic or lyric, does not present fragments of human experience, but formalized versions of it. The actions represented do not really take place; the persons, including the "I," do not exist outside the poem, or at least do not exist in the same way. Characters in literature have no extension in space or time beyond the limits of the work in which they appear; they have, on the other hand, a kind of extendability, a symbolic dimension, that the matter-of-fact persons of our acquaintance do not have. Together with the literary context in which they appear, they objectively represent something larger than any group of persons in actual life can ever objectively represent. That is, in "real life" we ascribe to persons a typicality or a symbolic function that they do not really have; there is no such thing as a typical American or a man of the people outside our speculations, there are only various men. In a novel or poem, however, the typicality of a man is objectively there, placed intentionally by the writer for us to see; his symbolic function, like his symbolic context, is an inseparable part of him.

The literary character is thus a formalization of our experience of actual human beings, as the literary context in which he appears is a formalization of more general human experience. And this is true for the lyric as well as for the drama. The frequent modern practice of making a clear distinction between a poet and his personae draws attention to the facts that art is formal and that a work of art—even a lyric poem—in which the poet is, as Wallace Stevens writes, "too exactly himself" is in danger of not being art at all. Stevens goes on:

> We do not say ourselves like that in poems.
> We say ourselves in syllables that rise
> From the floor, rising in speech we do not speak.
>
> [*CPWS*, 311]

We do not say anything directly, least of all ourselves. If we want to say ourselves, we make a formal structure whose import will be *us*.

The history of the word *persona*, extruding as it does into so many areas of human activity, offers a useful illustration of the ways in which human experience can be stylized, and helps to illuminate the common formality of drama and lyric. The word itself has served as an instrument for the formalization of grammatical, legal, religious, and psychological, as well as dramatic, relationships that define in part the human situation. The origin of the word is obscure. We know it is the Latin for an actor's mask, possibly derived from *personando* (sounding through). If this etymology is correct, it suggests that the name, *persona*, was originally given to the mouthpiece of the mask which concentrated and amplified the voice of the speaker. Later, by a series of metonymic developments, it came to signify the mask of the actor, then the actor's role, and eventually any distinctive personage or individuality.

The process by which the meaning of the word became generalized is worth inspecting in some detail. If it originally referred to the speaking part of the actor's mask, then it came to mean the whole mask because the function of speaking was presumably what distinguished dramatic masks from other kinds of masks: the mask was identified by reference to what was considered its most important property. Similarly, the role played by the masked actor came in time to be identified by *its* most important characteristic, the mask. For the mask of drama is not what it is in our ordinary usage, a device for disguising or hiding the face. On the contrary, the mask of drama, or of primitive dance, is clearly intended to reveal more than it hides, to affirm more than it obscures. In these forms the face is not important, but the stylized mask symbolizes, stands for, something—an attitude, a view of life, one aspect of the universe—which is of too great significance for the expressiveness of any human face to be able to convey.

If we follow the word's development further, we see that the person, too, is identified by *his* most important characteristic, his function as a player of roles in various kinds of dramas, or, rather, in certain formalized versions of aspects of human life, versions that are not literal dramas but perform functions similar to that which drama performs. In studying these versions we can profit most from a consideration of the analogies between the persons of grammar and the persons of the stage. It is appropriate that the distinctions between grammatical persons should be dramatic distinctions, for both grammar and drama are formalizations of the dynamics of human speech. Grammar distinguishes three persons: the speaker, the one spoken to, and the subject of discourse. Analysis of any statement to determine which entities are treated in the first, the second, and the third persons should reveal the point of view from which that particular statement is made. The use of grammatical persons is an index to the meaning of statements; it is a partial definition of the speaker's universe.

It was the Greeks rather than the Romans who perceived the similarity between dramatic dialogue and the situations which grammatical person describes. Their term for mask was *prosopon,* and when they gave the name to "the significant inflectional ending that we call the 'person' of the verb, they undoubtedly had the drama in view where persons really move as 'I' and 'you'." The Romans, following suit, used their own term for mask, *persona,* "there being," as Lucian remarked, "three persons just as in the comedies, the slanderer, the one slandered, and the one who hears the slander."[1]

But the fact that the borrowing of dramatic terms to indicate grammatical point of view seemed appropriate to the ancients suggests not merely that drama *uses* grammatical person in its talk on the stage; it implies, further, that the dramatic presentation of first, second, and third persons on the stage is a formal expression of the fundamental human state of affairs which grammatical person itself recognizes in a different but still formal way: Man talks. It is part of the nature of man that he speaks (with or without words) to other men, and that he speaks to other men about some part of their common experience. Grammatical person reflects the speaker's sense of this basic social feature of human personality. The speaker knows that he speaks, and that he speaks *to* someone *of* something. Without the connection between speaker and interlocutor which grammatical person formally expresses, no statement has meaning for human beings. "This rock is black," is a sentence that gives us no clue to its point of view. In order for the sentence to have any meaning, someone needs to know who is giving the information and to whom. But "I tell you this rock is black," where the entities designated by "I" and "you" are clear, conveys the human situation within which the information begins to have significance. Only in the form of the dialogue, in words or in gesture, can human meaning exist.

The dialogue, nevertheless, proceeds whether or not any "I" or "you" actually appears in speech. "This rock is black" is a perfectly meaningful sentence so long as the points of reference represented by "I," "you," and "it" are understood. The actual appearance of the pronoun or of inflected personal endings is only a formalization that makes a knowledge of the referents of the situation publicly available—just as the information itself is expressed in conventional symbols. The dialogue form may exist without receiving stylized expression in grammatical person. All social human activity is conducted in dialogue form, and perhaps all human meaning necessarily depends on this form for its existence. The use of grammatical person is merely a practical formulation of one of the conditions of human life.

But conversational language, itself a formalization

of whatever human impulses lie behind it, is only one of the media through which we talk to each other. Drama, indeed all of literature, is another; and a third is law. Like that of grammar the terminology of law borrows the word person from the stage. And appropriately so, for as Roman law consolidated into conventions, its procedure became highly formalized. To express the specific form of the human dialogue with which law is concerned—the meeting of two adversaries and the judgment as to the merits of their pleas—Roman terminology reverted to the language of the stage. The plaintiff is called *actor,* and the word *persona,* in its meaning as "role or part in a play" is given to plaintiff, defendant, and judge. In the *Institutiones* of Gaius, for example, we find the following sentence:

> Qui autem alieno nomine agit intentionem quidem ex persona domini sumit, condemnationem autem in suam personam convertit.[2]
>
> (But he who acts in another's name takes the accusation indeed from the person of his employer, but turns the condemnation against his own person.)

In the formalization of the human dialogue which is law, then, the attorney for the defense assumes the role (or mask) of the accused. When we say, therefore, that an attorney (he who turns toward) represents or "acts for" the plaintiff (the lamenting one) or the defendant (who wards off a blow), our language not only is filled with the ordinary metaphorical idiom of the stage, but suggests that the courtroom "drama" is a reflection, a formal expression, of the same human dialogue represented on the stage. Whereas grammatical person and the drama conventionalize the form of all human talk, the legal drama conventionalizes only one kind. Nevertheless, the legal ceremony that we call a trial is a dance of masked figures who perform the ritual steps necessary to present man in one of his aspects. The ritual in which all three masks play their roles functions as a formalized expression of one aspect of man as speaker.

We might go so far as to suggest that legal ritual expresses, among other aspects of man, his competitive impulses. Competition is clearly one of the forms that the human dialogue may take, and it finds formal expression not only in law but in such codified institutions as war, sports and games, business, and politics, as well as in the innumerable social codes of any civilization.[3] Like most of these other fields of ritual, legal procedure has its practical uses as a part of our literal environment. And like the others it has, as a stylization of a part of the human dialogue, its own emphases: most notably on the judging persona, a formal expression of the forces, conditions, or rules that give stability to any communal entity—the father, the umpire, the tribal chief, the President of the United States, or God.

As it happens, the word persona with all its original dramatic connotations has entered into only some of the many formalizations of the human dialogue. Most notably, perhaps, it holds an important position in the vocabulary of Christian theology. Both Latin- and Greek-speaking prelates of the early Church used their words for *mask* or *role* to describe the different forms of God—Father, Son, and Holy Ghost. The Greeks, to be sure, preferred the term *hypostasis,* but after the Council of Alexandria in 362 A.D., *persona, prosopon,* and *hypostasis* became equivalent terms. As Gregory Nazianzen wrote:

> A threefold light flashes upon us at the mention of God, threefold with respect to his peculiar characteristics, hypostases, or rather persons, one might say; but one-fold on the contrary when we regard the substance, that is, the godhead.[4]

It is difficult to say how many of the transient overtones of the word survived in the minds of the Church Fathers who established its use as a theological term. Certainly ancient writers had used the word to signify the various roles in life which a man might play. Thus Cicero says, using language that anticipates that of the later theological paradox:

> Tres personas unus solus sustineo summa animi aequitate, meam, adversarii, iudicis.[5]
>
> (It is with perfect mental balance that I, one and single, sustain three roles—my own, that of my opponent, and that of our judge.)

The paradoxical doctrine of the Trinity, which strikingly parallels the thought of Cicero, would inevitably encourage, no matter in what terms it was expressed, the proliferation of heresies. But even if we allow that the word *persona* had probably, by the time of its adoption into dogma, lost its close association with the theatre, its origin was still to cause trouble. In 1553 a certain Servetus was burned at the stake as a heretic for suggesting that "the three persons in the godhead were three functions in the sense of three roles."[6]

The borrowing of the stage word, in spite of the indirectness of the transaction, provides only one among many examples of the sense that the Church seems always to have had that religious ritual is a formalization of the dialogue between man and man, or, as the Church would put it, between God and man. The Persons in the Trinity are speakers, but to speak is to act: "In the beginning was the Word, and the Word was with God, and the Word was God." The sense that primitive peoples have always had of the significance, indeed the primacy, of speech in human history, is reflected in more sophisticated ritual. If we may not call these Persons masks of God, we may at least note the analogies between them and certain other masks frequently appearing, as it happens, also in threes: the three persons of grammar; Lucian's slanderer, slandered one, and hearer of slander; the plaintiff, defendant, and judge of court drama; and, in the modern anatomy of the human person, the ego, the id, and the superego.[7] In all these groups of persons there is, first, a self; second, an entity to which the self relates in a *particular* way; and, third, a miscellaneous environmental entity whose relation to the first two members of the triad is more general, more impersonal, and yet essential, a persona, a mask, which compresses all the rest of the universe into temporary relevance.

As we view all these groups together, recognizing the distortion as we distort them (for in historical Catholicism God is not usually conceived of as a central self to whom Christ and the Holy Ghost bear second- and third-person relationships; nor do we think of the plaintiff as the central self in any legal dialogue, having been trained to think of the judge or the jury or the court itself as central), we can, I think, see what really is happening in all these relationships. Man speaks to man about the human situation; he speaks as Father to Son; as accuser to accused; as slanderer to the hearer of slander; as "I" to "you"; and even as ego to id. In some of these relationships the "speaking" does not necessarily take the form of speech, yet the human and creative sense of communication is present, or, rather, the sense on the part of the first person of significant relationship with the second, different in kind and in degree of specificity from relationships with the third. At least one conscious view is present in each relationship; and the *point of view* is that of the first person, the "I."

Whether or not God or the ego objectively exists is still under debate; but these other first persons certainly do not. There is no such thing as "I" or a slanderer or a plaintiff; there are only specific men who may assume, among others, these particular formal roles. One suspects, hence, that all these persons are, in the contexts in which they appear, only formalized versions of aspects of human reality, means of objectifying the multiple and disparate life that all men share. Whether or not they speak, appear in court, take part in a drama, talk to themselves, create the cosmos, or perform other similar actions that are similarly formalized, all men exist in a world in which at most moments they have significant and attention-demanding correspondence with other beings, and in which at these moments they have more distant and indirect relationships with other things or persons. Such relationships are of numerous kinds, and their formalizations will be multitudinous. Language, perhaps, gives us one of the basic formulae for treating these relationships. But even language, as we have seen, is not direct. Grammatical person, like, in their own ways, Christian, psychological, and dramatic person, merely gives linguistic recognition—and hence symbolic expression—to an actual state of affairs.

Perhaps all human consciousness is a formalization of unconscious impulses and feelings. If so, then human thought is feeling formalized, and language is the medium through which feeling becomes thought. But once language exists, it becomes an almost natural part of our environment; once thought exists, it thinks about itself as well as serving its expressive purpose. Both language and thought, whatever their origins, whatever the deeper human realities that lead to their creation, are symbolic systems that function simultaneously as means of stating the informational content of the human dialogue, as means of expressing the feelings of human beings, and as means of underlining the existence of human dialogue. That is, every sentence, every unit of thought, contains not only information and an emotional tone, but also an indication of point of view. Language and thought are the means by which man says to man: "I tell you this thing is true, and I feel this way about it."

In actual speech, however, these three elements—fact, tone, point of view—may be muted, may even vanish. Point of view is usually only implied. The tone that reveals the speaker's attitude is often so built into the presentation of the information that we cannot specifically locate it, or it may be expressed rather by gesture or silent implication than in linguistic form. The information itself may not be explicitly given but only hinted at, to be read by the perceptive between the lines of actually spoken words. These three functions of speech may thus be fulfilled only indirectly: the information, the point of view from which the information is given, and the emotional import of the information, may all be deprived of literal expression, and yet be expressed by implication.

We recognize this indirection as the method of irony, of certain kinds of satire, and even of a great deal of other literature. We find that the import of great drama—what the writer is really "saying" to the reader—is embodied in the action (including speech) and its tone, not in any explicit general statements spoken by any of the characters. In fact, we read all literature nowadays between the lines, feeling that explicit statements by the writer are, if we take them out of context, merely more or less graceful speech, but in context serve only to reinforce that far more momentous significance that the work as a whole represents. No statement in a literary work of art is literally true, although it might be true if withdrawn from the work and tested by extrinsic standards. For literature seems to be based on the reader's ability, frequently drawn on in daily linguistic and nonlinguistic life, to interpolate and extrapolate significance where none explicitly appears. Literature must work in this way, for "significance" is so much a function of human feeling that only the whole work of art, or a part of it read with a sense of the whole, can qualify as an expression of that feeling. Language is only the comparatively toneless tool, developed by man's capacity for symbolization, which literature uses to give formal expression to human feeling.

For all of literature is in its form a stylization of the same human dialogue that, as a whole or in certain of its aspects, receives stylized treatment also in grammar, legal procedure, and Christian theology. Each of these activities has a literal dimension and a symbolic dimension: speech occurs in a form that is variously expressive of the ways in which human beings must, as they are human, talk to one another. The speech of literature, too, contains these different dimensions—the speech of the lyric as well as that of drama.

In drama the first persona addresses a second and may talk about a third. When the second speaks, he becomes the first persona, and his interlocutor becomes the second, for whoever speaks *is* the first persona and whoever is spoken to is the second. The third may become the second by being addressed or the first by speaking, and the first two may become the third if they are referred to by other speakers. The personae of the stage, like the persons of ordinary life, shift their grammatical roles, and the audience takes in the action first from one point of view, then from another, grasping the "I-ness" of each persona at the same time as it regards each of them from outside as a "he." For the persona, the mask, the person, is a role, a point of view, which any man may assume; the different *personae* of grammar and the stage are roles among which a man may move.

But while the *dramatis personae* alternate as speakers, each of them represents a fairly consistent point of view, a role or part that is signalized by the mask and parallel devices of costume, gesture, and speech. On the stage these points of view, these attitudes, find themselves in conflicts (to be in relation is to be in conflict) with one another, conflicts that are sometimes in the foreground of the action (as in the I-you of dialogue), sometimes in the background (he, she, it, they). The conflict among points of view, however, is complicated by the implied comment on all the points of view which the playwright makes from his omniscient point of view (somewhat as the judge in the courtroom triad resolves the conflict between two other persons). In this process the writer relegates all the masks and all the surface action of the play to third-person position. The discretion with which he selects certain points of view for presentation, and his skill in arranging and controlling them, give to each of them in turn a deeper significance, for in any final analysis the meaning of each presented point of view, of each person, is formulable only with reference to the total hypostasis, the structure of meaning which the play as a whole represents: the playwright's voice, his deepest lyrical person, *his* point of view.

For there are always two levels of speech in a work of literature—that on which the characters speak to each other, to themselves, to an implied audience, or to God, and that on which the writer speaks to us. In the lyric poem more than in any other genre these levels tend to become confused. We can sense rather easily the presence of the two levels in a fairly formal lyric, say a love sonnet. On the surface we can read the following personae:

1st person: singer of love song
2d person: singer's mistress
3d person: singer's love for mistress

On the deeper level of the poem the poet talks to us:

1st person: composer of song
2d person: we as readers or hearers
3d person: human passion, one aspect of the human world

Even if the poet is in love to distraction, the poem is always finally addressed to us. Beyond the plot, beyond the characters, even beyond any expressed didactic statements, the writer is telling us something, giving us his view of life or of some part of life. But such a view, requiring for its full formulation these particular events, situations, emotions, and tones, can never be expressed by any "I" within the poem. The poet's point of view is always larger than that of his "I," for the "I," like the other surface materials of the poem, is only a conventional element in a symbolic context that serves as the formal expression of the poet's view of reality. If the point of view of the poet is not larger than that of his "I," what we have is not a poem but transcribed and polished talk, a fragment of *a* human dialogue instead of a stylization of *the* human dialogue.

All this holds true for the lyric as well as for other, apparently less "personal," kinds of literature. We tend to think of the lyric as stating "directly" the poet's feelings or thoughts; but, in fact, definitions of the lyric by reference to its content are mostly recent. J. E. Spingarn tells us:

> . . . during the Renaissance there was no systematic lyric theory. Those who discussed it at all gave most of their attention to its formal structure, its style, and especially the conceit it contained. . . . [For them] the real question at issue . . . is merely that of external form.[8]

And Raymond Macdonald Alden writes:

> . . . the word lyric is used both in a general and a more particular sense, having gradually been extended from its original meaning—a poem to be *sung* by a single singer—to include all poetry expressing *subjectively* the emotion of the poet or those whom he represents.[9]

The more formal definition—"a poem to be *sung* by a single singer"—shows us how clearly the lyric is to be contrasted with the drama, in which several "singers" take part. From this point of view lyric might include epic and, more loosely, all fiction not actually dramatized on a stage, for even in those stories told in turn by different characters a single voice, presumably that of the author, is the voice we hear throughout.

But even if we accept in spirit the restriction of "lyric" to those poems that express "*subjectively* the emotion of the poet or those whom he represents," we find that the poems themselves do not express anything subjectively but the poet's view of life, the feelings that are communicated on the second and deeper level of the poem. On the immediate and literal level the poem presents *objectively* "the emotion of the poet or those whom he represents." If it were not so, the poem would not be a poem. As in the drama, as in fiction, the action of the lyric must function as a trope, a figure, a mask, an affirmation in symbolic terms of whatever it is that the poet, most deeply, is telling us. The speech of literature is different in kind from that of ordinary talk, and the lyric, no less than the drama, is a stylized abstraction of the human dialogue, not an instance of it.

III

But precisely what is a poetic persona? In spite of frequent references to the term in modern criticism, how it functions in poems is still far from clear. Most of those who speak of personae and masks treat them as evasions or obfuscations of the self rather than as revelations of more significant aspects of reality. Discussions of Swift or of Blake sometimes imply that the use of masks represents a lapse of the writer's integrity, that the author is "hiding," and that the device of the persona is at best dubiously poetic. Such writers usually try to "get behind" the masks to "the man," to the historical human being whose beliefs, education, prejudices, and impressions belie the masks and throw light on the "real" meaning of the work. Research along this line has the merit of all biographical inquiry directed toward the illumination of literature, but it often overlooks or distorts the specific literary purposes that the mask is designed not to evade but to fulfill. Only very recently have a small number of articles and books begun to examine the use of personae as a satirical or ironic technique; yet, although at least one persona is present in every work of literature, modern criticism contains hardly a remark on the use of personae as a fundamental literary device.[10]

Literature is made up of words, composed by writers and spoken by personae. In some works the distinction between poet and speaker is obvious; in others it seems an extravagance to call attention to a distinction so thin that it can hardly be said to exist. Its existence is nevertheless a matter of fact. The persona may share much with his creator—a point of view, an attitude toward life, certain historical circumstances, certain intellectual qualities; but the persona is part of the poem, and the poet exists outside it. The author dies; the persona has a permanently potential existence, realized whenever the work in which he appears is read. However skillfully the poet may try to effect an identity between himself and his persona, the task is hopeless, for he and what he has created exist on different metaphysical levels. Mainly because the speaker is in the poem, not behind it—though he may be behind the events of the poem, not in them—he cannot quite be identified with the maker of the whole poem, speaker and all. The speaker is wholly a product, and only apparently a source.

But even the speaker is, like living creatures, a far from simple entity. In the first place, personae often reflect the complexity, the contradictions, the intricate inconsistencies we know to be characteristic of human beings —reflect them in compressed and economical form, perhaps, but may succeed nevertheless in suggesting them. Of all this every critic is aware: the place of character in literature is acknowledged by everyone to be of great importance. At the same time we know almost nothing of those characters we call personae, the characters who speak the actual words of poems.

For personae, although they often partake of the

richness of characterization open to all literary personages, are constituted differently from the rest because of their role as speakers. In fact, whereas characters who do not speak at all, whose words and actions are described rather than confessed, exist on a relatively simple artistic level, personae exist on two or three levels at once. In one sense, it can be said that in any poem there is not one persona but several. Coexistent and almost inextricably entangled with one another are several points of view each of which qualifies and complicates the autonomy of the others, and none of which is ever quite identical with the poet.

Indeed, at the very source of poetry lies a persona whom no poet would identify with himself but whom, as he appears in every poem, the poet necessarily disclaims. Inseparable from literature is its use of rhetorical devices, and inseparable from their use is the art of dissimulation. Although rhetoric may be thought of as an aid to the forceful telling of truth, it has often been treated and recognized as a systematic discipline for lying with effect. Most rhetorical devices serve the poet by asserting what is not literally or apparently true, with the excuse that an ulterior truth may be usefully enforced by departures from apparent truth. Similes pretend that two objects resemble each other usually because of a few comparable qualities, but Burns knew that a rose and his love were far more different than alike. Metaphors carry the falsehood even further through the pretense that the two vastly dissimilar entities are identical. Personification, onomatopeia, metonymy, hyperbole, oxymoron, and many traditional poetic devices are all tricks that, whatever their sanctification by the instinctive processes of human thought, deliberately misstate the "facts" of human experience. Of course, there is a sense in which some of these misstatements may be true. The use of "sail" for "ship" conforms to certain visual facts: when we see the sail we know that we have sighted a ship. And there are mornings when it is more precise to say instead of "dawn,"

> But, look, the morn, in russet mantle clad,
> Walks o'er the dew of yon high eastern hill.

Such usages possess the validation not only of conventional practice but also of a part of the mind which may have as good a right to the term "truth" as any other part of the mind. The poet nevertheless knows that the morning is not a human being dressed in a mantle; he is aware that his assertion is at odds with conventionally received categories; he is further aware that his audience both knows the assertion is not literally true and will accept it as "true" in another, more important way. The scientific verifiability of the fact is nothing compared with the poetic rightness of the image. But the two worlds are in conflict. The poet in his use of language goes further beyond the bounds of ordinary "sense" than most people publicly dare, but he also restrains himself from going too far. The further the image goes in its falsification or distortion of acceptable fact, the greater must be the poet's power to curb this anarchic force and compel it to take its place in an intelligible design. The poet thus plays a double role: through one persona he explores regions of knowledge whose laws are outside conventional speculative thought; through another persona he retrieves the first persona from a mere chaos of associations and employs the associations in a design governed by the syntactical and logical connections necessary to articulate thought.

The exploring persona is thus always falsifying the "facts," and if we see him as a consistent creation of the poet, we can detect in him a kind of elemental persona. This persona is not only, like the innocent dupe that we see in Gulliver or Prufrock, fumbling in his grasp of the structure of moral reality; he is consistently ignorant even of the socially accepted versions of the physical bases of the universe. One object is continually transformed into another, people and things are confused; the organic and the inorganic, the living and the dead, the terrestrial and the cosmic, the human and the nonhuman, endlessly exchange their properties. Living largely in a sensory world, this persona associates phenomena according to their textural and accidental impact on his senses and fails to honor or even recognize the categories of scientific, moral, religious, and social "fact." Judged by the conventions of organized society, this elemental poetic persona is incompetent, savage, lunatic. And even when other personae are superimposed upon him and speak through him with a superior awareness of civilized conventions of knowledge and conduct, the elemental persona persists in his distortions of all the achievements of speculative thought.

Richard Wilbur's poem, "Praise in Summer," treats this doubleness of the poet rather humorously:

> Obscurely yet most surely called to praise,
> As sometimes summer calls us all, I said
> The hills are heavens full of branching ways
> Where star-nosed moles fly overhead the dead;
> I said the trees are mines in air, I said
> See how the sparrow burrows in the sky!
> And then I wondered why this mad *instead*
> Perverts our praise to uncreation, why
> Such savor's in this wrenching things awry.
> Does sense so stale that it must needs derange
> The world to know it? To a praiseful eye
> Should it not be enough of fresh and strange
> That trees grow green, that moles can course in
> clay,
> And sparrows sweep the ceiling of our day?[11]

Let loose, the elemental persona here threatens continually to go out of control, in spite of the exertions of his more sober counterpart. Yet the existence of the sonnet tells us that the elemental persona is really in custody. The form of the poem is superior to the struggle: appearances notwithstanding, order triumphs over anarchy.

The extravagant assertions of the elemental persona would no more satisfy the writer than the reader if the assertions were taken in isolation and as literally true. But they are not so taken; their deliberate extravagance is part of a pose that every writer assumes and every experienced reader knows he will assume. For above the level of the elemental persona is another that includes it and bears to the author a relation similar to that which the elemental persona bears to it. This is the civilized persona, the persona who, in spite of his excursions into evident ignorance of cultural agreements, is really aware of conventional manners and morality—sometimes only confusedly aware, like Gulliver, but sometimes, as in *The Prelude,* aware to the point of wisdom.

Such is the conventional persona of literature, the speaker whom we recognize, the voice that we expect to hear. Were we to meet directly, in words, no one but the elemental persona, we should hardly call our experience a poem. But the flashes of his appearance are subject to the civilized control, usually unconscious, of the more continuous personage of which he is a part. The elemental persona comes and goes, and really only makes up a part of the superior personality of the speaker. Whether we regard the elemental persona as an aspect of his more civilized counterpart, or as an almost autonomous and distinct personage, the language used in literature includes two opposite points of view—that which orders experience through conventional rational structures, and that which orders experience through conventional affective structures. Perhaps in every phrase of literature both views are present, but especially in those usages we call rhetorical; and perhaps the rational persona always dominates the affective persona. When Burns writes,

My love is like a red, red rose,

he uses the orderly syntax of rational discourse to make an affective assertion; he uses the order of reason to support an order of feeling. But the rational order is always present, or nearly always, in every affective image. The very words are products of reason if their meanings are commonly known, and so are the syntactical connections between them. Even if Burns had written, "My love, rose," he would be relying, for the communication of his unscientific identification, on the conventional denotative meanings of words, punctuation, and word order—in fact, on the rationally apprehended structure of English, the medium of his art.

Both the affective import of rhetorical devices and the rational systems in which they figure and which they alter, are part of the person of the speaker of every poem. He may not fully understand what he is doing, for he himself is part of the poem, and the poem as a whole makes out of its combinations of affective and rational structures another structure basically affective but which also has import for the rational structures of civilization (given an audience). Every persona is, in the first instance at least, a part of the rational structure of the poem in which he appears; he locates for the reader a point of view from which the words he speaks have significance. And, as the speaker of the words of his poem, he serves us as one element of its unity. Even the most detached reporter implies through his choice of subject and his choice of words an attitude toward what he reports, and in good writing this attitude will be consistent enough to be intelligible as a point of view.

But while the words of a poem are spoken by a persona, they are also in some sense spoken by the poet. They issue from two different mouths simultaneously—from the mouth of the mask and from the mouth of the man who wears the mask. Yet even this distinction is not quite accurate. For the poet is not present in the poem; whatever we sense of him there is partly contrived, partly beyond the power of deliberation to contrive. What reader, from his view of the intelligence behind the verse of Shelley or the fiction of Conrad, would ever guess that the smooth stylist spoke with a thick Polish accent, or that the intense poet was ever less than intense? The poet not only contrives a speaker for his poems; he also contrives for himself a personality that the reader can abstract from the poem. Some aspects of the writer are omitted, others are added, so that the idea of the poet which comes to us from the poem is often a representation not of what the poet is but of what he thinks he is or would like to be or cannot help being. Yet, however this picture of the poet relates to the actual man, it is this intelligence that we take to define the perspective of the poem.

Neither the persona nor the poet we abstract from the poem is ever quite the actual man: so much is clear. Nevertheless, we do abstract a picture of the poet from every poem, a picture made up partly of qualities the poet wishes us to credit him with, partly of qualities he does not deliberately display. In satire, probably, the poet's arrangement of this picture is most conscious because the satiric poet detaches himself from his persona. Whatever the mode—satiric invective, high or low burlesque, or simple irony—the writer, as we say, assumes an attitude he does not share; that is, the persona voices ideas and a point of view with which the author is not, or not wholly, in sympathy. But the attitude that contrasts with that of the persona is not the attitude of the poet himself, but the face of the poet as he himself has prepared it. In light satire the author shows us a sly, laughing face; in satiric invective a twinkling eye qualifies the glance of scorn; behind Rabelais' works we sense a man of boundless vitality and imagination; behind Swift's a relentless, subtle, indefatigable earnest intelligence. How accurate these or other pictures of satirists may be as we derive them from their works the biographer may illuminate, but though the portrait may be veracious in spirit, it must always be incomplete, must always be different in detail if not in emphasis from the man himself.

In lyrics, too, the dimensions of the poet's personality *in* his poem are subtly various. In a sense, all that is in the poem reveals what he is; in another sense, every particular character—indeed, every momentary attitude, every habit of reflection, every turn of phrase—is drawn from what the poet is, from what he has observed in others as well as from what he has observed in himself, and from much both within and outside him that he has never consciously observed. But in addition to all the characters whose actions are reported by an observer (and which may often be approximate projections into a third-person dimension of the poet's idea of himself), there are two specific personalities that define every work of art: that of the speaker and that of the implicit poet. Neither of these is the living poet himself; they are divided from him by the same chasm that differentiates art from life. But either of them may serve, and may be intended to serve, as approximate representations of the poet himself.

In fact, the poet in the poem, the intelligence with which the poet identifies himself and with which the reader is invited to identify himself, may exist anywhere, and at more than one point, along a sort of sliding scale between the persona and the whole poem. Poet and reader meet together at that point of vision from which the meaning of the poem becomes most clear and most comprehensive. But since different ages have different views of meaning and of poems, their location of the poet in the poem will vary. While the persona always serves as an apparatus for giving a perspective on the surface actions and events of the poem, the area of vision at which poet and reader meet provides a perspective from which the actions and events can be interpreted as meaningful in a world of meanings. In general, ante-Romantic, Romantic, and post-

Romantic poetry choose different locations for the poet in the poem and hence for the reader's guide to its meaning.

IV

Throughout the long tradition of the English lyric down to the Romantic era, the persona of poems maintains a fairly consistent identity. When the troubadours of Provence sent jongleurs to sing their songs for them, they established a tradition that the lyric followed for many centuries. The practice is again reminiscent of drama: as the playwright composes words for the actor to speak through a mask, so the lyric poet composes a song for the jongleur to sing. The jongleur is the lyric persona, and he sings through masks of his own, the different roles—lover, mourner, panegyrist—which compound his role as singer. As the origins of the tradition become obscured, the disparity between singer and poet decreases, and the lyric persona comes to be identifiable as singer or poet, or poet as singer. Nevertheless, the sense in which the persona is a poet must be carefully discriminated. The "I" of most English lyric poems is identified by his vocation of song, not by his physical and social existence as a man. The lyric persona is man singing, man as composer or singer of songs.

When he turns his music to specific human activities and events, and takes on more specific human modifications in order to play his roles, the singer does not forget that he *is* a singer. The several conventional kinds of lyrics place the singer in relation to conventional subjects—to love, to death, to his country. And what he says of these subjects will conform largely to the audience's expectations derived from experience of other singers; through song the singer confirms and deepens the audience's conceptions of love or death. Thus, a love sonnet does not present man in love, but man singing of love; an elegy is not a presentation of man feeling about death, but of man singing about death. The poet appears not as man undergoing experiences but as man singing about his experiences. The Renaissance lyric persona repeatedly refers to himself as a poet or singer, in effect as man in his role of celebrant of human reality. Herrick's well-known lines exceed others only in articulateness:

> I sing of brooks, of blossoms, birds, and bowers:
> Of April, May, of June, and July flowers.
> I sing of May-poles, hock-carts, wassails, wakes,
> Of bridegrooms, brides, and of their bridal cakes.
> I write of youth, of love, and have access
> By these, to sing of cleanly wantonness.

This, as Herrick tells us in its title, is the "argument" of his work, and it is the argument, too, of the traditional lyric. The poet is a singer. Whatever else he is remains irrelevant. He never, or very rarely, appears as a full man, participating in all the variety of life as other men do, with private interests and private business of his own. His only business is song; whatever he celebrates, he celebrates in his role as singer. For brooks and blossoms unsung are different from brooks and blossoms sung. The singing of them is an assertion of their value, a transportation of them into a dimension peculiar to the sung.

In a sense, all that the poet sings is apostrophe. He *names* objects, people, events, and through his conceits, his arrangement of his poetic materials, he names their meaning. By naming them he acquires a mastery over them; by fixing them in a song he asserts their meaning. They have, in a way, only a limited vitality until they are sung; sung, their life is permanent as the song itself is permanent. The immortality that Elizabethan sonnets promise to bestow on their subjects is typical of the lyric; whatever the persona touches springs into everlasting life. By the act of singing, the persona arouses the sleeping world into the special significance available only to what is sung.

But the poet cannot sing everything at once. And the conventions of his age largely dictate the areas to which he may apply his song, and the manner of application. The singer assumes a further role—lover, mourner, panegyrist, storyteller—often in a particular setting—pastoral, urban, courtly, domestic—and speaks words appropriate to role and setting. All roles, if anatomized, are complex enough, but most lyric poems contain singers whose attitudes are stylized according to contemporary conventions. The conventional persona of traditional lyrics is man singing on one or more subjects in one or more situations: he celebrates a marriage, a birth, or a triumph; he mourns a man, a cause, or an age; he sings a tale; he announces or examines his love for another human being. Often the persona engages in more than one of these activities, but he is always fulfilling some such permanent human roles as these, compounded with his role as singer. The poet's training in the conventions of his age teaches him a practical understanding of the nature of these roles and certain techniques by which he can manage the roles skillfully. Both the roles and the special techniques (as well as his vocabulary, his sentence structure, and much else in his work) are largely chosen for the writer by conventional practice, but every good poet develops not only his own slightly different techniques but also his own variations on the traditional roles. There are perceptible shades of difference between the singing lovers of Sidney, Spenser, Shakespeare, and Donne; in fact, the persona often varies his attitudes from one poem to another. But all the singers are lovers, and their attitudes, their points of view, are closely, even when perversely, related to contemporary ideas of love and lovers and to contemporary experience of lovers in poems.

Other recognizable genres employ singers in other recognizable roles. The singer of patriotic songs is a patriot; the singer of dirges is a mourner; the singer of reflective poems is a reflective man. Every conventional kind largely defines, and is largely defined by, the role of the singer; which comes first is hard to say, for the two work together. As the poem is all words, the words define simultaneously the singer and the nature of his present activity; a role itself *is* a kind of conduct rather than a kind of man. The assumption of any role is an act of limitation and compression; it is a means to the focusing of human intelligence on a specific category of human experience. As the poem does not cover all of life, so the "I" is not the singer in all his possible human roles. But both, along with other poetic elements, are narrowed: the "I" to denote the singer in the specific role of lover or mourner, the subject matter to love or death, the tone to certain limits appropriate to both subject and speaker, the diction to certain similarly appropriate limits. Within these bounds the poet can range widely; almost every conceivable attitude toward love and death can be and has been taken. But conventions tend to make possible the more concrete renderings of feelings about any subject. No singer is all men in all moods, as no poem tells all about life. As each poem defines itself in its progress, so it defines and limits its singer as well. Every poem that emerges as satirical excludes from its coverage an acceptance of man as straightforwardly meditative; every poem consistently nonsatirical excludes from its coverage satirical man. The speaker's role and the genre define themselves together and are recognizable in terms of similar roles and genres that readers have already met.

But along with the generic conventions, personae are subject to the conventions of eras. In every age the poet chooses as the "I" of most of its lyric poems a figure whose qualities and whose implied social position are acceptable to a contemporary audience. Whatever the circumstantial eccentricities of the speaker—be he Trojan or Chinese, for example, in an English poem—his values must be not too far different from those of his audience, and his moral universe must be roughly theirs. There must exist a correspondence, a possibility of communication, between speaker and audience. They must speak the same language in more senses than one. The "I" of many old ballads, for example, is a folk storyteller who, like his audience, knows of strangeness abroad in the world, of suddenness in love and death, of shock and grief and lapses in the clarity of causes. He claims no superiority to his audience; and his point of view, his attitude toward life, his view of its pungent realities, are all available to his listeners—are, perhaps, theirs before they are his.

In more consciously literary writing the speaker of the lyric is similarly on a level with his audience. Lyric poetry in the Provençal tradition puts forward a singer who is, in the main, a courtier. Such poetry is intended for a courtly audience and meets the expectations of its readers or hearers. The qualities and social status of lyric personae, however, change in England as the political and economic center of gravity shifts from the aristocracy to the middle class. The courtly "I" becomes more and more bourgeois even in Elizabethan days and continues its downward path through the seventeenth and eighteenth centuries. In weakened form the courtly poetry persists, and its courtly persona still meets the expectations of a courtly reader, still claims no superiority over him. But the "I" employed by the metaphysical poets is clearly lower in social standing than that of Wyatt or Surrey or Spenser or Shakespeare, not because the poet is of lower rank, but because the audience is. By the time of Dryden and Pope the singer is most typically a well-bred man of sense; by the end of their era the man of taste and tact vies with the man of feeling, and in the great Romantic upheaval it is the man of feeling and insight who, still a gentleman, becomes the chief poetic persona.

None of these roles is a simple role. The courtier is made up of a thousand qualities, as we know from the Renaissance manuals on his training, and his substance is modified from century to century, even from reign to reign. The persona who speaks courtly poetry changes along with the general conception of the courtier: Sidney's does not speak like Guillaume of Poitiers', Suckling's is different from Sidney's, and Rochester's from Suckling's. Individual poets differ further, just as their individual conceptions of a courtier are bound to differ. Suckling, Lovelace, Carew, and their fellow poets show us different, but compatible, views of the courtier through the poems they allow their personae to speak. The role, like all other stylized roles, is subject to infinite variation, to the point where it ceases to be the role of the courtier and becomes recognizable as a different mask—in Shenstone, for example, the singer who was once a courtier has become a rather Horatian country gentleman.

In general, the singer is a member, not necessarily ideal or even exemplary, of that social class to which most of the audience belong, or of a social class or other kind of group which the poet expects his audience at least to honor: the personae of Milton and Burns, for example, speak poems warmly admired by readers outside the religious or social milieux of the personae. But, by and large, what the audience is, the persona will be also; at least in the great mass of English poetry before 1700 the persona is on a level with his audience, seldom superior to it, and speaks out of an assumed common knowledge of the ways of the world and of God.

This equality of reader and persona is a constant in most poetry. Neither Homer nor Virgil nor Dante allow their personae to talk down to their readers. Poets have occasionally been arrogant, but they have usually known that the showmanship required to get a hearing for a poem includes the task of persuading the reader of his equality with, or superiority to, the speaker. The subtly inserted compliments so often paid by poets to their patrons are evidence not of the poet's servility but of his graciousness, not of the indignity of his office but of his grasp of the reader's humanity. Any public speaker, not excepting a poet, must win his audience's good will. Even satiric invective relies on the reader to see through the extravagance of the persona's wordplay and consequently to sense his own superiority. It is thus not surprising that the poet is, in early English criticism, rarely thought of as a prophet, however his office is dignified in theory. Only in the seventeenth century does a magisterial note, a tone of authority and self-importance, make serious encroachments on the formerly modest persona; and the great practitioner is, beyond all others, Milton. In Milton's usage the poet is not merely a singer at a court of nobles, or a courtier on an idle day; the poet has high and sacred duties, not at all dissimilar to those of the ancient prophets, to recast the moral life and re-order the social structure.

This change in the conception of the poet has serious consequences also for the "I" of poems. In earlier lyrics the "I" could remain a singer, and the poet could allow the singer to affirm reality by singing it. In this affirmation the poet takes no pains either to identify his own person with that of his persona or to disclaim any such identification. In fact, the poet is out of it; once he has set his singer to singing, the man himself can withdraw. But an echo of the man remains in the poem. Whatever the subject, the reader may perceive an emergence of meaning, of meaning principally contained in its very assertion. Praise of a virtuous or beautiful person may lack justification in reality; but the truth or falsity of the persona's judgments has little effect on the poem. For the poem asserts the value of singing virtue and beauty, or the value of singing corruption and sin; and to this value the specific instance is, as itself, irrelevant. The poet and reader meet at the level of the whole poem, together appreciative of the beauty of the song and of the sung quality of the subject.

This is not to say that lyric poets consciously detach themselves from their singers. It seems clear that for most poets of the Renaissance the distinction between poet and singer is not deliberately drawn. But the "I" of their poems never emerges as a circumstantially complete portrait of the poet; we find at most only a turn of mind, a general temperament, which appears to be that of the poet. But all this gradually changes as the lyric persona becomes more and more a specific man and less and less man singing. By the early nineteenth century the typical persona has become individual and particular, has ceased to be "a singer" and become "the poet"—*this* poet, the poet writing the poem, "I" in all its literal force.

V

Since the confusion about the identity of the speaker revolves around the possible denotations of the word "I" and the inevitable use of an "I" in literary art, it is not surprising that when the external conditions of the Provençal division of labor between poet and singer were forgotten,[12] the lyric "I" gradually came to stand more and more for the poet himself. In fact, it is doubtful if in practice the poet ever completely detaches himself from his persona. Although the "I" is fundamentally a singer, a mask through which the poet examines reality, the poet necessarily draws from his own experience in establishing the song of his singer. And because in any linguistic symbolism the word "I" is a center of ambiguity, even the poet may become understandably confused as to who it is that actually speaks his poems. Thus Herrick, in the rest of the poem quoted above, goes on listing the matter of his song, but in the last two lines becomes something more than a singer:

> I sing of dews, of rains, and piece by piece
> Of balm, of oil, of spice, and ambergris.
> I sing of times trans-shifting; and I write
> How roses first came red, and lilies white.
> I write of groves, of twilights, and I sing
> The court of Mab, and of the Fairy King.
> I write of hell; I sing (and ever shall)
> Of heaven, and hope to have it after all.

All the persona's activity until the last two lines is present-tense activity, for his office requires him only to sing or to write (the offices of poet and singer clearly merge as singer and writer become almost interchangeable). Under the conditions of the lyric as an apostrophe, as a naming of subjects in song, the present tense is perfectly appropriate. The celebration of the parts of the world is a subjection of them to the magic process of poetry, through which they become things sung, different from things unsung. The singer in the poem, through the pure apostrophe, also acquires the agelessness, the elemental stylization, of what he sings —the world, in fact, is pure song. But the agelessness suffers a jar in the penultimate line when the singer refers to his future intentions. As they are still confined to his role of singer, they do not violently disturb the picture. But the last line quite destroys the view of the singer which we have so far built up, or rather conveys the persona from the dimension of a mask to the dimension of actual life:

> I sing (and ever shall)
> Of heaven, and hope to have it after all.

"After all" does not mean "after a career of singing," but "after my life as a man." Heaven is not for singers, but for men. And our realization that this singer is not man singing but *a* man singing alters our interpretation of the whole poem. A man, not a singer, has been speaking all the time.

We have only to look back a half century to the sonnets of Shakespeare to see how the singer, though filled with the accidents of humanity, remains a singer through all his human experiences. Our criticism has taught us to regard the final couplet of the Shakespearean sonnet as a flaw, and if we take the sonnet as a personal statement by the poet, the too neat plunk of the couplet must seem inevitably distressing. But if we regard the speaker of the sonnets as a singer, not as Shakespeare, the final couplet retrieves the singer from the manhood, the loverhood, which he has assumed as a mask for the first twelve lines, and restores him to his role as singer. The couplet reminds us that the song is a song and that the love that it portrays is not really the love of the poet, but an emblem of all love. The first twelve lines of Sonnet 30, for example, show us vividly the experience of memory:

> When to the sessions of sweet silent thought
> I summon up remembrance of things past,
> I sigh the lack of many a thing I sought,
> And with old woes new wail my dear time's waste.
> Then can I drown an eye, unus'd to flow,
> For precious friends hid in death's dateless night,
> And weep afresh love's long since cancell'd woe,
> And moan th' expense of many a vanish'd sight.
> Then can I grieve at grievances foregone,
> And heavily from woe to woe tell o'er
> The sad account of fore-bemoaned moan,
> Which I new pay as if not paid before.

If the poem ended here, or went on in similar fashion, its structure would resemble, even with the contrived judicial conceit, that of an infinite number of later poems, in which the poet's purpose is to recount his own experience as an instance of all experience, and thus to celebrate experience itself rather than experience sung. But the poem finishes:

> But if the while I think on thee, dear friend,
> All losses are restor'd and sorrows end.

Read a Romantic structure into the sonnet, read man into the singer, and the final couplet is inadequate to balance the convincing melancholy of the three quatrains. But the couplet reminds us that the speaker is only a singer, singing of friendship and its effect on unhappy memories. The memories are not, after all, real, though the description of them is applicable to any man; the friendship, too, is not real, though its description may fit real friendships. The poet is not giving us an example of what it is to be alive and to go through one experience or another; he is not dramatizing experience as central in human reality. He is singing a song. Within the song's structure the persona may be as vivid, as particular, as "human," as the poet can make him; indeed, these qualities may strengthen the illusion of reality which is part of the poem's structure. But just as the power of the *play* depends, as De Quincey partially saw, on the audience's becoming free of the illusion, on their understanding that it is "revels" that take place on the stage, so in the sonnet the reader must perceive that the experiences presented are emblems of reality, not reality itself.

Thus in his comedies Shakespeare makes abundantly clear the illusiveness of what he has presented, not only by occasional overt references to it, but also by the traditional artificial endings, which approximate in function that of the sonnet's closing couplet. In tragedy, similarly, the business of the state resumes, and if it resumes under a cloud, it is the cloud of a sharpened consciousness of good and evil and the shadowiness of human and cosmic forces, the dense "airy nothing" for which the poet has deliberately contrived "A local habitation and a name." But the life does resume; the actors were all spirits; the theatre and all its settings and scenes "dissolve." Concrete reality has never existed in poem or play; all that appears in them "imagination bodies forth." And like the actor, the sonnet's persona, if we try to reach him as a man, to apprehend his human reality, is "melted into air, into thin air," the air out of whose "nothing" the poet has created the illusion of the persona's actuality.

The final couplet of the sonnet serves to emphasize this illusive quality of all the experiences portrayed in the poem. The poet's office is thus a double one: to create the illusion and then to dispel it. The mask of drama and dance fulfills a similar function. While the masked actor speaks his words and performs his ritual gestures and actions, the audience must retain its awareness both of the individual character the actor gives to his role and of the fact that it *is* a role. In the drama or lyric lacking the actual physical equipment of the mask but aiming to produce the same illusionment and disillusionment, the structure of play or poem must assume a heavy burden.

But why does the poet not give without qualification, as Romantic poets do, the impression of an actual man going through actual experiences? Because the poet's aim is not to have the reader undergo a direct apprehension of human experience, but to have him undergo an apprehension of *sung* human experience. Attention is drawn not away from the experience presented, but *toward* the fact of its being sung. The poet tells us of the importance of poetry. The craft itself has meaning for people. To sing of something is valuable, and it is valuable independently of its results. The rationalizations about poetry's relation to history and philosophy with which Renaissance critical theory confronts us fail to convince the modern reader. For the Renaissance poem is ultimately not concerned with any truth but the truth of singing. Every poem is an assertion of the value of singing, at the same time that it is a realization of that value. The characteristic description of the poet as an artisan, a craftsman, is much to the point here. The poet's job is to make a poem, to sing his song with all the skill at his command. The result of his workmanship is the poem, the play, the song, in which he himself appears doubly: explicitly, in the mask of the persona-singer, and, implicitly, as the skilled artisan behind the song. The audience in turn meets him at both points—hears him as the persona, and, more importantly, admires the craftsmanship of the whole song.

Only the philosophical terms of our own day provide consistent explanations for the Renaissance sense of the value of singing. Our own insights into the nature and purposes of such symbolic activities as art allow us to see how singing is meaning, and that to sing reality is to formulate it by a method that carries with it its own system of significance. Neither Renaissance critics, however, nor those of subsequent centuries had available to them the kinds of ideas needed to justify the continuation of a poetry making deliberately clear its own illusive quality. As the demand for truth in poetry becomes more strident, the "I" gradually loses its aspect of mask and takes on the characteristics of actual human selves. Satire temporarily provides one means of evading the problem, since the "I" of satire must be detached from the poet. Comedy, too, survives for a while as a dramatic form because its structure demands a final release from the audience's sense that the occurrences on the stage really take place. As the eighteenth and nineteenth centuries come on, the apparently straightforward poetic forms—tragedy as well as lyric verse—continue to lose their consciousness that they present experience as illusion. Tragedy drowns in its now single dimension; melodrama, purporting to present actuality, gradually takes over the stage; even comedy, in order to keep its distance from actuality, a distance that the audience finds it increasingly hard to grant, must verge on farce; and lyric poems rely more and more on the literal self of the poet to speak truth.

Thus, instead of the poet's speaking in the role of a

singer who in turn takes up other roles, the middleman slowly disappears, and the poet takes up the roles directly. Probably something of the poet-as-singer always remains, if only implied by the verse form, just as something of the poet-as-man has always inhabited the singer. But the emphasis changes. As the poet lends more of his own human qualities to the persona, the presence of the poet in the persona becomes more substantial. And as the lyric ceases to call attention to its own artificiality, the persona becomes more central in its structure; it grows harder to detect the poet above his work, and easier to see him *in* it in his persona. Donne in his love lyrics assumes quite directly the role of lover, and the intermediate role of singer obtrudes but little. Milton's personal sonnets show aspects of Milton the man, and the famous opening of Book III in *Paradise Lost* displays a persona who, though still a singer, is Milton himself as poet:

> Thus with the Year
> Seasons return, but not to me returns
> Day, or the sweet approach of Ev'n or Morn,
> Or sight of vernal bloom, or Summers Rose,
> Or flocks, or herds, or human face divine;
> But cloud in stead, and ever-during dark
> Surrounds me, from the chearful waies of men
> Cut off, and for the Book of knowledg fair
> Presented with a Universal blanc
> Of Natures works to mee expung'd and ras'd,
> And wisdome at one entrance quite shut out.
> So much the rather thou Celestial light
> Shine inward, and the mind through all her powers
> Irradiate, there plant eyes, all mist from thence
> Purge and disperse, that I may see and tell
> Of things invisible to mortal sight.

The singer has in this passage given way to the poet; instead of man in his ritual role as poet, we find here this poet, this man, this singer—Milton.

That the solidity of poetic personae increases from Milton to Wordsworth hardly needs argument. Whereas the personae of the metaphysicals and of Milton's shorter poems speak largely without scenery of any kind, other seventeenth-century poets, notably Denham, begin to place their lyric personae in more particular settings. With this development the voice of the persona becomes less disembodied, more like the voice of an actual man. A corresponding and contributing development gradually elaborates the figure of the poet as a man who by the end of the eighteenth century is superior to all other men in the qualities that most command admiration—sensibility and imaginative power. Thus, outside the poem the poet becomes the model of an experiencing self, while within the poem he is identified with the persona who, increasingly particularized, represents man in one role or another.

Although earlier poets had been working toward it for a long time, it was only in the poetry of the Romantics that the persona arrived at a degree of particularization which changed his essential nature. In Renaissance lyrics the persona as singer typically comments on human experience, sings it, names it, treats it in the special manner of poems. In the typical Romantic lyric the persona goes through an experience, recounting it as he proceeds. In fact, as Robert Langbaum points out in *The Poetry of Experience* (New York, 1957), the latter is the typical pattern of poetry since the Romantics. The personae of Wordsworth, Keats, Tennyson, Browning, Eliot, Yeats, are usually presented as undergoing experiences, not singing them. Nevertheless, the nineteenth century has special distinguishing characteristics and must be dealt with separately.

As the circumstantial identification of the persona reaches a high point in the Romantic lyric, so does the participation of the poet in his persona. Not only do poets explicitly present themselves as personae—the technique is too common throughout the great Romantic poets to require illustration—but they are also frequently to be associated with the points of view of third-person characters (Manfred, Endymion, the Poet of *Alastor*) into whose experiences the poet has clearly projected his own attitudes and expects his readers to project theirs. That is, the self whose activities comprise the poem becomes the principal meeting place of poet and reader in the poem. As the persona shares the characteristics of the Poet—a man, as Wordsworth's *Preface* tells us, "endowed with more lively sensibility, more enthusiasm and tenderness, who has a greater knowledge of human nature, and a more comprehensive soul than are supposed to be common among mankind"—and as the persona, too, often shares the general and even specific circumstances of the individual poet, the reader is invited to share not only the perspective of the persona but also his attitudes. The greater part of what we might call the reader's (and the poet's) projective energy is directed into the self of the persona. Inevitably, some is left over so that the poet and the reader can meet together in appreciation of the whole poem. But the emphasis rests on the experience presented and, as part of that experience, the wisdom acquired from it; the emphasis does not rest on the poem itself.

The special virtue that resides for man in singing, thus gives way, as major implication of poems, to the special virtue that resides for man in experiencing, in experiencing life not songs. And far from the poet's pointing out that the persona and his activities are merely illusory, the poet attempts to strengthen the illusion, indeed to persuade the reader of its virtual reality. The more "real" the experience seems, the better; if the reader takes it for literal reporting, splendid! The distinction between phenomenal actuality and what appears in poems begins to be blurred. Poetry almost becomes history or biography because it reports what is taken to be literal truth. As everything within the poem comes more and more to be a reproduction of actual things and people outside it, as the "I" becomes increasingly the poet himself, the poem runs the risk of losing the peculiar properties of poems.

Sung experience, in this process, becomes valuable insofar as it is *like* unsung experience. The song imparts no peculiar value to the events and people contained within it; rather, the poet assures us that the events and people already have a value that the poem merely reports. Of course the poet makes a selection among people and events, and he allows experiences to be reproduced in the poem at their most forceful. But the emphasis is on what the poet reproduces or appears to reproduce, on its quality as fact outside the poem and not on its virtue as something sung. This is the pretense that underlies all love poetry, but in the typical Renaissance lyric it is recognizably a pretense. The value of a conventional sonnet turns not on the special properties of the subject but on the way in which the compliment is managed, and if possible on the resultant deepening of the reader's insight into the general topic of discussion. The Romantic lyric keeps the general applicability—it must, to remain a poem—but it does so by extending into a type something that is actual, not by actualizing something that convention has already marked as typical. The poet enters the poem and becomes the type of man; in the Renaissance lyric the conventional persona was particularized by accretions from the poet's personality.

In most nineteenth-century poems the self is central in, and definitive of, reality. As experience makes men what they are, poems reveal selves either undergoing significant experiences or having undergone them. Eventually, they may come to arrange the universe in ways that make it coherent, a task that earlier heroes had largely had done for them by conventional systems of thought. But in the nineteenth century value is something that desperately needs reëstablishing.[13] And as the only source of value is the human self, the self must arrange and define reality. Its experiences thus are part of the process of definition, but the experiences center in the experiencer. In "Dejection: An Ode" Coleridge tells us:

> Ah! from the soul itself must issue forth
> A light, a glory, a fair luminous cloud
> Enveloping the earth—
> And from the soul itself must there be sent
> A sweet and potent voice, of its own birth,
> Of all sweet sounds the life and element.

The incapacity to undergo the significant experiences required if the self is to create its world is the source of Coleridge's dejection—itself, as it turns out paradoxically, a significant experience. In fact, nineteenth-century literature characteristically presents a self searching through significant experiences for meanings that he finds within himself. The external world functions as an objectified setting for this internal struggle; the circumstanced persona serves as an instance of the questing soul. By knowing this experiencer, especially by knowing him from within, by being him for the duration of the poem, the reader, too, can undergo his significant experience and hence grasp reality. As the self's experiences confer value on the world, so the persona's experiences confer value on the poem, and poet and reader meet at that point in the poem where they can best elicit value—within the experiencing persona.

At the same time, because this poetry is concerned with extraordinary experiences—experiences that, however common in occurrence, have special significance for the experiencing self—the self, too, has a habit of being an extraordinary man. Not everyone, not even Coleridge very often, is qualified to undergo these significant but demanding experiences and realizations. The persona practically *has* to be a poet in order to respond appropriately to his experiences. If experience is to *be* significant, the persona must have the capacity to respond to it with suitable force and to see it as meaningful. Feeling will do the one, imagination takes care of the other. But in possessing these extraordinary qualifications, the persona becomes a hero as well as a protagonist. His speech accordingly takes on an exalted tone; his manner becomes superb. He addresses the reader from a height that his reader can only dream of attaining, or can attain only through a wholehearted projection of himself into the persona. Persona and reader are no longer on an equal footing, no longer share a diction and a tone. Conscious of the superiority of his experiences and capacities, the persona must speak in elevated language, a language of exclamation and apostrophe, continually passionate, continually above the usual language of his audience. He and they cannot be on equal terms, for he is not one of them: he is an exemplar, a poet, a hero. He is significance speaking to ordinariness. In self-defense ordinariness must identify itself with significance.

In all this the dramatic monclogue of Browning makes a momentous dent. Not only do his personae customarily use tones of ordinary talk, but they are not heroes, only protagonists, and their virtues are considerably qualified by their faults. They are still experiencers, but separate from poet and reader, who meet together mainly not in the persona but somewhere beyond him. Robert Langbaum writes:

> It can be said of the dramatic monologue generally that there is at work in it a consciousness, whether intellectual or historical, beyond what the speaker can lay claim to. This consciousness is the mark of the poet's projection into the poem; and is also the pole which attracts our projection, since we find in it the counterpart of our own consciousness.[14]

As Langbaum points out, we sympathize with a Browning persona at the same time that we withhold our judgment of him; that is, we enter his world, even his consciousness, to see what it is like; he gives us a perspective on his own situation. But the moral implications of the historical and intellectual facts that he ignores broaden our perspective on that situation. The reader, like the poet, apprehends the persona in two ways at once. And the purpose of the poem is to present for apprehension a particular instance of human personality. By apprehending the persona we achieve our reading of the poem.

What happens here is, in a way, the beginning of modern poetry. The easy tone with which Browning's persona addresses the reader (or is overheard) reflects the kind of experience he undergoes and the poetic purposes he serves. Andrea, the Duke, even Saint Praxed's Bishop, Fra Lippo Lippi, and others do not undergo significant experiences as we hear them speak. True, they *have* undergone some, but the moment at which we see them is a moment of significant being, not of significant action or choice. We might almost say that they are significant instances of life, not instances of significant life; and this is to say that we draw the meaning out of their presentation, not out of their being or acting. Instead of our seeing people at moments significant for *them*, we see them at moments ordinary to them but of special significance for *us*.

Through this apparently simple change in perspective the poet withdraws both himself and the reader from an identification with the persona, and locates the poem's meaning in an awareness superior to that of the speaker. Not the experience of the persona, but the experience of understanding him, is what the poet invites the reader to share. Through their significant perspective poet and reader converge to grasp that part of the world which is under examination. The emphasis, to be sure, is still on the object examined; the poet shows us what his speaker is. It remains for later poets to carry the process a step further and thus to create a poetry sensibly different even from Browning's: Eliot, Yeats, Pound, and others, though still intent on the reality they present, will continue, even when they present a persona undergoing experience significant for *him,* to withdraw the poet from the persona and to move, even to the level of the poem itself, the point at which the reader and the poet meet. The reader's apprehension of the *poem* will, in effect, be the significant experience presented, as it had been in the Renaissance.

But it is Browning's dramatic monologue that begins this poetic development. To "My Last Duchess" we are not allowed to respond by saying only, "What an admirable self the Duke is!" or even "What an extraordinary person he is!" we must also say, "How cleverly Browning manages the Duke!" By separating poet and persona, by making the reader's sympathetic identification with the persona tentative and instrumental instead of virtually absolute, Browning reminds the reader that the poem is a poem, a work of art, a fiction, and that there is a craftsman behind it. And the poet whom we identify as existing somewhere in the poem tends no longer to be definable as an actual man, a human personality, hardly even as a temperament, but rather as an artistic intelligence, a disembodied consciousness, saying in effect to the reader, "Look at what I have made!"

VI

The more we learn of literature, the surer we become that it undergoes almost continuous change, and that its changes are slow, inconsistent, and dependent for interpretation on later times. The poems written in any year, like the people who write them, are at different stages of what future critics and scholars may see as coherent development. No poet in his time can clearly foresee which of his poems will begin an important movement, for an apparently conservative tendency may to much later minds appear as the significant revolution of an age, whereas a daring innovation may one day seem a tasteless variation on a mode already trite. Byron, defender of the poetic tradition of Dryden and Pope, would be abashed to find that we consider him in the revolutionary company of Wordsworth and Coleridge; and the Imagists would suffer an equal shock to know that while they conducted their crusade, poetry was modernizing itself in more important ways, and that only forty years later Imagists and Georgians seem far more alike than different.

In fact, we can hardly plumb the full meaning of any competent poet until his poetic progeny further extend and define his tradition. Although we like to think that we respond to intelligent artistry in any shape, we do so more easily when the shape is bracketed by imitators and influences. Thus, the work of Eliot and Yeats has, in our own day, been illuminated by our familiarity with later poetry that they have influenced, but Ezra Pound's *The Cantos,* if not all his work taken as a whole, remains puzzling because no more recent poet has substantially followed his poetic. Although the Pound tradition does not exist, there seems to be good reason to believe that it will develop, and that the critics of the next century will give him more of understanding than we can afford even of sympathy.

Because innovations in poetry are so elusive, even poets themselves cannot fully realize what they have started. And in tracing the tendencies of any poetic technique, the critic must often appear to attribute to a poet a greater consciousness of his craft than the poet could possibly have had. Shakespeare, Wordsworth, and Browning treated their personae as they did for reasons that they surely never formulated in full, and with results and implications that they could not possibly have known. Yet they knew something, and most English poets have tried to indicate, directly or indirectly, why they have written as they did. And our knowledge of their successors helps us also to understand their criticism, which in turn illuminates the poetry.

In our own time we recognize a wide variety of poetic approaches among an extraordinary number of practicing poets. To generalize about them requires an accurate sense of which poetry will emerge as important and which will emerge as trivial. Those poets we usually think of as most modern—Eliot, Yeats, Pound, Stevens, Auden, Thomas, and others who are indebted to these—seem in many respects to define a contemporary tradition. But poets like Frost, Sandburg, Jeffers, Muir, Graves, and Masefield, though different from each other, seem yet more different from the "modernists." The generalizations equally applicable to both these groups are not at all numerous, and few writers on modern poetry feel comfortable in dealing with them together. The present study will be, in this respect, no more enterprising than most. The differences between the two groups, however, become somewhat clearer when we look at their personae.

In the first place, one characteristic seems to hold good for both groups. Virtually every modern poet in virtually every poem uses a persona who addresses the reader on terms of virtual equality, using diction and tones that the reader himself might use. The poet has descended from his nineteenth-century heights to chat with the reader, or to tell him, in tones basically casual, what he knows. Although Coleridge, Keats, and even Wordsworth occasionally treat the reader as an equal, no one in the nineteenth century approaches Browning for his easy air, his geniality, his assumption of common ground between persona and reader. In modern poems, too, the dizzy ecstasies and sublime heights may appear, but they appear very rarely as the dominant tone. Rather, they exist as human possibilities among other tones possible to men. But the dominant tone of modern poetry is that of casual talk—in Frost or in Eliot, in Auden or in Graves, in Yeats or in Jeffers.

The persona, therefore, no longer shares the lofty and superior qualities of the nineteenth-century version of the poet. He tends to be rather like other men, perhaps just enough more perceptive than they to feel that his insights and experiences are worth recording. But as a New England neighbor talking to New England neighbors, a literary man talking to literary men, a man on a quest talking to men on their quests, the modern persona has become a representative rather than an ideal man. In effect, the Poet has lost his sublime characteristics and no longer feels that his own specific temperamental qualities need to be stressed.

At the same time, the persona usually remains a man rather than a singer; he is an actual human being, with hopes of heaven and fears of hell, often in a particular setting and undergoing specific experiences. But the difference between the poets we call modern and those we call traditional (whatever the absurdities of such a terminology) mainly lies in the extent to which the poet's projective energy remains with the persona, or the extent to which it is withdrawn from the persona and meets the reader's at another level, especially at the level of the total poem. Poets like Frost, Jeffers, Graves, Muir, and even Spender and Day Lewis characteristically give us personae from whose points of view we tend to see the whole poem. Eliot, Yeats, Pound, and their comrades characteristically employ the method of the dramatic monologue: they ask us to sympathize with personae to obtain a superficial understanding of the events of the poem, but they insist that we meet the poet's passionate intelligence at a point where we can more fully understand the poetic context of the persona and of all the events of the poem.

To some extent all poetry does this, but in modern times the dramatic monologue has been the principal instrument for transferring emphasis from persona to poem, and those poets who have cared to effect this change in emphasis have persistently used the dramatic monologue. The monologue offers the poet the opportunity to withdraw from the persona, to present as speaker a limited character with whom neither poet nor reader can be ultimately identified. The reader is allowed to feel morally or intellectually superior to the persona, or at least to feel that he has access to more information—in short, he sees the persona in a context of which the latter is unaware, and he recognizes that this implied context is also a part of the poem. He may even recognize further that the poem itself, in providing the context, performs a service far beyond the capacity of the persona.

The persona, in short, is diminished in stature to the point where he can no longer represent fully the spirit of the poet. In Browning's dramatic monologues the personae usually reveal their faults casually, and often unconsciously, to the reader, and they do not possess what the reader possesses—a full perspective on their characters. But their hearts are often in the right place, the burden of what they say is often valid, and they themselves possess qualities that win our sympathy or admiration. We wonder at the vigor of the Duke, we sympathize with the erring humanity of Andrea, we laugh with pleasure at the rich lusts of the dying Bishop of Saint Praxed's. Modern poets often follow a similar pattern, consistently diminishing the persona until his qualifications to speak truth or represent virtue are ambiguous.

For to depart from the Romantic magisterial "I" is not so easy as it looks. The poet who sets up in its place a simple and unpretentious persona, like that of Housman and some of the Georgians, may produce bathos: to pretend to be simple may be the worst pretentiousness of all. Nevertheless, only by coming down to the level of the reader, by convincing him that the persona, however complex, is approachable, can the persona presume to speak at all. In many poems, therefore, the modern poet, fresh from his Heine, his Corbière, his Laforgue, as well as his Browning, diminishes his persona by mocking him. In some poems—"Prufrock," for example, or "Gerontion"—the mockery is final; the insufficiency of the persona is too great to allow him to see anything very straight, or to take an admired attitude toward what he does see straight. The more typical technique, however, consists in establishing a mockery that, whether it is achieved by the persona himself or by the poet, makes the "I" thoroughly human, possessed of enough moral weaknesses so that the reader can listen to his views without feeling oppressed. In effect, the best path into the modern reader's heart is by way of weakness, not strength.

This diminution of the persona can be accomplished through the use of various techniques, the least effective of which is probably the frank disclaimer of knowledge. Instead of the persona's telling us directly how naïve and foolish he is, the poet can present him as combining naïveté and foolishness with wisdom and good sense. Richard Eberhart, for example, begins "The Groundhog" with these lines:

> In June, amid the golden fields,
> I saw a groundhog lying dead.
> Dead lay he; my senses shook,
> And mind outshot our naked frailty.[15]

Throughout these four lines the expectations of the reader are repeatedly shaken; the persona changes form continually, mixing a variety of dictions with apparent innocence in an attempt to say something fundamentally valid. The poem begins like a traditional celebration of summer and of personal experience with it. But the flatness of the second line and its bald content disperse any thought of Lowell's rare day in June and lead the reader to believe that the persona is a simple, straightforward man merely describing the facts as they occurred: "This is the setting; this is what I saw." If setting and scene do not fit together in the usual "poetic" way, that is not the fault of the reporter. But dimly conscious of the discrepancy, he goes on to rephrase the fact in somewhat more poetic terms, using a traditional inversion, which, however, manages with its dissonant vowels to emphasize the bald fact before him: the emptiness of the inversion reflects the apparent meaninglessness of the event and the inability of the persona to grasp its significance. He is stumped. Then in new kinds of phrases he describes his momentary dizziness and his instant speculation about the nature of death. From his mixture of dictions we are confirmed in our sense of the linguistic innocence of the persona; his mixing of metaphors in the last line (in a figure we cannot visualize) reinforces our impression, as does the use of the cliché, naked frailty. At the same time we become aware that behind the apparent indecorousness of this eclectic language there is a certain odd propriety; the wandering among dictions is a part of the search for any certainty. And the fourth line is not only intelligent but pointedly in contrast with the ideas presented in the other lines. The sudden juxtaposition of the living and the dead, of human mental powers with the inevitability of human death, makes us see the previously bald scene with new meaning. The persona may be an ingénu (the typical role of satirical personae), but he is also worth listening to. He is not all ingénu; he is partly wise. And, as readers, we can listen the more readily to his wisdom because we feel superior to his folly.

"The Groundhog" presents a self undergoing a significant experience, and with this self and his experience the reader is urged to sympathize. But the ambiguity of the self has two implications: in the first place, it asserts, like other techniques of juxtaposition familiar in modern poems, the complexity of the human world. Nothing exists absolutely; qualification is the first principle of intelligence and wisdom. Because all that we know contains its own contradictions, all that we learn must arise out of understanding of those contradictions. In the second place, the ambiguity of the self invites the reader to look beyond the persona for what we call the center of the poem. In the poetic structure characteristically used by modernist poets at least, the self, though still (and presumably eternally) the observing instrument and even the scene of conflict, is no longer the center of significance.

The following chapters attempt, along with an examination of the personae of Eliot, Yeats, and Pound, to show that the center of the reality which their poems present is not the self but something else. In Browning's dramatic monologues the self is central, but the attention of the reader is called to the superior consciousness that speaks through the poem. Eliot, Yeats, and Pound pursue this technique so far that they eventually write a different *kind* of poetry. In their poems the self serves only as a unifying surface point of view, but the center of the poem is the poem itself taken as a whole, taken as a vision of reality, as the *poet's* vision. It is not merely at the level at which poet and reader apprehend the persona but at the level at which they apprehend the poem, that the reader's consciousness fully meets the poet's. Browning meets his reader at a point where they can survey the poet's material; Eliot, Yeats, and Pound meet their readers at a point where they can survey the poet's treatment of his material—his song.

For the self to these poets is not opposed to the world, nor creative of it, but part of a world to whose reality it contributes and which alters it in turn. Both self and all that is external to the self are involved, implicated, in each other; in fact, not only does the external affect oneself, but, in the last analysis, the external is also within. And, conversely, the world is permeated with the presence of man, its most important element; his past and even his future are part of the world's present, intricately interwoven into its fundamental structure. Value, consequently, lies less in the anatomy of experience than in the anatomy of the mutually mirroring self-and-world. To discern one is to discern the other. To present an experience is thus to present all experience as it is at the moment. For "all experience" is human reality, is the world around us, a world to which the collective and private experiences of selves give its color, its tone, and hence its value. In poems at least, the world is valuable *as* experience.

To formulate such a world in poems, the poet employs personae as instances of experiencing selves, but the reader at the same time undergoes a more complex experience. Since the poem shadows forth a world valuable as experience, the reader experiences the poem as a world. Within this world exist two selves—the persona and the poet. While the persona leads us through his experiences, through that world of his from which he is hardly to be distinguished because he and it so fully define each other (as Prufrock, Gerontion, Irish Yeats, Crazy Jane, Pound in *The Cantos* are embedded in their worlds), the poet himself takes us through the ordered experience of the poem. In every phrase, in every rhythm, in every unit of the poem we feel the force of the poet's presence; in the poem as a whole we feel his passionate intelligence pounding disparate experience into the permanence of poetic form. And set beside this monumental consciousness fixed in the stasis of the poem itself, the persona is only a piece of the rock out of which the whole has been formed. He and his experiences serve as a kind of Jacobean subplot, adumbrating and reflecting the more powerful experience that the fuller poem is.

Furthermore, because the poem is now a world valuable as experience, it once again asserts the value of singing, or, in more usable modern terms, the value of writing poems. The emphasis, to be sure, now rests on singing as an epitome of experience, not on singing as an instrument of meaning; but since experience at its best *is* meaning, the Renaissance and modern aesthetics seem, in this respect at least, close together. The Renaissance lyricist asserted the value of the song as a means of transforming externally significant phenomena into artistic significance. Eliot, Yeats, and Pound do the same. Both groups of poets treat the song less as a means of enriching or reporting phenomenal reality than as a thing valuable "in itself." Behind the song of both eras stands the craftsman who has made the song, assuming in one age the role of singer, in the other a variety of more immediate human roles. But in both songs we detect the poet's voice, the voice of the craftsman who is responsible for the song. In a sense, the song, not the persona, is the poet's mask, for it is there, in the whole song, that we find the poet to be most fully present. The persona, the *embodied* representative of the poet in his work, distracts our attention from the fact of the poem as the embodiment grows more lifelike and as we interpret it to be a facsimile of the poet himself; the *disembodied* consciousness of the poet, discernible in every poem but almost dangerously obscured in the nineteenth century by the emphatic appearance of the poet in the persona, represents the full *person* of the poet more deeply. In Eliot, Yeats, and Pound, as they themselves see and say in different ways, it is the poem, not the speaker, through which the poet speaks, and which therefore serves as his persona.

2

Eliot: The Transformation of a Personality

To UNDERSTAND the personae of any writer we must first have an idea of the characters who inhabit the world of his poetry, for it is from these characters that the personae, the speakers, will be drawn. Some writers, perhaps because of the genres they usually explore, use few characters, others use many; some use vaguely defined people, others define them with great precision; some poets change their tactics in the course of their career, greatly increasing or decreasing the number or the exactness of their people, without usually abandoning the qualities that hold all the characters together. For every poet we sense a range of persons who represent in part the poet's view of human life.

Probably on no other score has Eliot's work been so condemned as for its choice and treatment of people. Yet the number of characters who, directly or by immediately understood allusion, make their way into his poems is phenomenal. Because of the peculiar allusive structure of his verse, it is difficult to draw a line between who is and who is not actually *in* his poems. In one sense, only the old man, his boy, and his housekeeper inhabit the world of "Gerontion"; in a second sense, it is inhabited also by the jew, Christ, Mr. Silvero, Hakagawa, Madame de Tornquist, Fräulein von Kulp,

De Bailhache, Fresca, and Mrs. Cammel; in a third sense, it is inhabited by characters whom the old man's phrasing recalls—Vindici, Beatrice of *The Changeling*, Everyman, Tennyson's Ulysses, Judas, and others, all of whom are, when the allusions are perceived, hardly more shadowy than the second-level characters or, indeed, than the boy, the housekeeper, or even the old man himself. In the same way *The Waste Land* employs a small army of characters either present or recalled, all of whom contribute to our impression of Eliot's treatment of people. And other poems, especially those written no later than 1922, introduce people almost as multitudinously as Hardy's *The Dynasts*.

But the peculiarity of number is not the only distinguishing mark of Eliot's characters. Their kind of actuality is rather different from that of any other poet's people. In the first place, the poet cares little for their individual qualities; what he cares about is their relationship to certain enduring archetypal roles. They act, consequently, if they act at all, in conformity to the demands of their roles rather than from what we should call personal motives. The details of their talk, of their manners, of their gestures, are idiosyncratic rather of their roles than of themselves. The shifting of the candles by Madame de Tornquist, the entrance of Doris from the bath, the successive actions of the typist and the clerk, all reflect nothing individual in these persons—no charming inconsistency, no personal diabolism—but are clearly ritual actions that they perform in order to fulfill their roles in a ritual drama.

It is this ritual aspect of his characters which makes them so different from the people we usually know. We are accustomed to thinking of people as individuals, or at least as types familiar to our culture, but, for the purposes of his poetry at least, Eliot gives us people whose archetypal roles characterize them more fully than do their cultural and individual peculiarities. Occasionally what we think of as a human face breaks through the archetypal mist—Prufrock, the Lady, sometimes even Sweeney, and the poet himself in *Four Quartets*. Such characters as these are exhibited in their culture in somewhat more detail; the poet permits them greater local definition. But they still retain their roles in the ritual drama, still speak and act in response to ritual demands. The typical character in Eliot's poetry is like the Lady at the beginning of "A Game of Chess," identified only by her room and the objects it contains, by her perfume and by the disembodied words she utters. We see everything in her setting but of her nothing but her hair. Naturally enough: *she* is not important; what is important is the role that she plays, a role defined more fully by her environment than by anything peculiar to herself.

At the same time, though, the contemporaneity of the archetypal is stressed. Most of Eliot's characters are drawn from modern European culture, and much of the point in their actions lies in the juxtapositions within them of contemporary and eternal human qualities. This arrangement enables Eliot to present the modern world as merely one of an infinite number of disguises that permanent human reality may wear. And just as individual qualities are slighted, so the culturally accidental fuses into the humanly essential.

Since Eliot's characters do not usually receive substantial individuality, and since even their cultural characteristics give way to their human ritual roles, they are often unstable. Different persons who play the same archetypal role tend to "melt" into one another, and even the different roles merge into abstract humanity. In Eliot's verse a comparison of one character with another is often, to a degree unusual even in poetry, an identification; because of the scanty individuation, the distinctions between persons and between levels of actuality are unstable. Agamemnon appears not merely as a figure comparable to Sweeney; he *is* Sweeney, or at least the two men are not altogether distinct. The women in *The Waste Land* are all one woman, as Eliot tells us plainly, the men all one man, and "the two sexes meet in Tiresias," who is man in the archetypal role of quester. Personality is shadowy and tentative; the human, not the individual, occupies almost all the poet's attention. The characters are like unconscious immortals who, in the fashion of Tiresias, change shape, setting, culture from age to age and repeatedly perform the same ritualistic functions in Egypt, in Greece, in England, from behind masks that betray nothing of the distinctive face.

Among all the possible roles, Eliot has chosen mainly to portray that of the quester, man in his role as seeker for meaning, truth, reality, virtue, the good life. All the events of Eliot's verse take their meaning from their relationship to this quest, and all the characters must be interpreted according to the ways in which they fulfill this role. Those who continue to pursue the goal either have or do not have the requisite qualifications; those who fail to pursue it at all, or who give up the pursuit, are damned. Virtually every character can be evaluated in terms of his reference to this central situation. Since the pursuit may be attempted through various human activities—mainly love, poetry, political and economic activity (history), and religion—some characters are treated only or mainly in terms of the search as it may be made through one of these areas. Most of the women of *The Waste Land*, for example, are reprehensible for their degrading attitudes toward human love, which in Eliot's verse never turns out to be a very profitable path for the quester. The quester in *Ash Wednesday* works through religion, in *Four Quartets* through several of the possible activities, but in *The Waste Land* the protagonist's search is more general: it is *the* quest, whatever its specific form.

This use of poetry reflects Eliot's beliefs about the nature of human life. He sees man as primarily engaged in a quest, seeking, through the various modes of conventional activity, satisfactory terms on which to live with the cosmos. But as characters melt into each other, so selves melt into the world that they define. Value in Eliot's verse resides not in the self or any qualities thereof, but in the reciprocal working out of a relationship between self and world. They define one another in such a way that the self's action alone cannot establish value. The world around the self enters into it as fully as the self enters into the world, so that the establishment of a satisfactory relationship between them is a reciprocal enterprise, hardly manageable by the self alone, which must know when to take action and when to wait for action to be taken:

> Teach us to care and not to care
> Teach us to sit still [*CPP*, 67]

Passion and perception are insufficient equipment for the quest, because the quest is really a quest of the world to come to terms with all its parts. It is in this coming to terms that value lies, in the working out of a form of conduct, a process signified by ritual disciplines and realized in the making of a poem.

His poetry is thus concerned with *being*, rather than presenting, a form symbolic of the conditions of human life. In a sense, the world, not the poet, writes the poem, just as the world, not the self, achieves value at one moment or another. Since value is still inseparable from human selves, however, they must form the principle instances through the articulation of which poems come to *be*. And the reciprocal process, dramatized in the fact of the poem but also dramatized in the instances of the poem, can be approached from several points of view. Sometimes speakers tell us their stories and so reveal their moral situations; sometimes they direct our attention to other selves and other parts of the world. But always in revealing one they reveal the other. The confession of experience reveals the world implicated in the experience; the observation of a world reveals the implicated self of the observer.

But specific human personalities are only one dimension of Eliot's treatment of people. Any objective account of the world must show the presence not only of human selves but also of the marks they have left upon it. Any physical setting, such as those of *Four Quartets,* is suffused with the almost palpable meaning (obscure as it may be) of the consciousnesses that have lived or worked there or merely passed through. Earth, air, water, and fire are so suffused with the human quest that the quest has become an objectively discernible aspect of these elements. History is present, and so is the future. And as men transform the physical universe into something objectively more than physical, that something more enters again into every subjective self. Each pervades the other in a constantly renewing and re-ordering process.

If, then, the poem is to be a reproduction of that process, it must not limit its account of human personality to the occurrence of specific personages. The poem itself is an instance of the world, or rather a verbal symbol of it. It, too, is a palpable physical reality, but, like the world, it is suffused with the mark of both past and present human consciousness. Thus the poem recapitulates the tradition of poems both by containing specific allusions and by echoing in form and tone the poetic achievements of the past. It further reproduces the humanness omnipresent in the world by the multiplicity of authors and characters whom it recalls or vaguely echoes and who give to the world its own specific character. At the same time, a single present directing consciousness fills the poem and moves among its words with the same powers and limitations with which men move about the world. The presence of the poet in the poem is as objective and as difficult to formulate as the presence of man in the world. But each gives to what he inhabits the color and the tone that we recognize as its effect. The poem symbolizes the world, and the poet fulfills the coördinate role of man.

II

To portray his specific personages, Eliot employs in his early work a technique comparable to sculpture; his later work recalls the motion picture. Like Browning's dramatic monologues, Eliot's early poems present personae whose motions are arrested. Like the figures on Keats's urn, these personae are caught permanently in certain attitudes. The poems are portraits of souls in various conditions, of souls who do not advance or recede in their quest. As in Dante's *Inferno,* all progress in the poems is not of the soul portrayed, but of the reader and poet toward a sense of the fixity of that soul's condition. The personae do not grow wiser but only more confirmed in the attitudes with which they began; such events as take place only reinforce their positions. Prufrock, the protagonist of "Portrait of a Lady," Gerontion, and the "I" of most of the other poems unify the world they present by the attitudes they take toward it, attitudes that do not change but which it is part of the purpose of each poem merely to present.

The same is true of much of Eliot's later work—of the Ariel poems, *The Waste Land, Ash Wednesday,* and *Four Quartets.* Yet in these poems the poet is concerned to present souls rather in attitudes of movement than in attitudes of stasis. The points of development portrayed are sometimes phases, sometimes moments of change. Certainly Eliot's technique remains largely the same—he is always essaying an unmoving portrait of a soul. But the souls of the early speakers remain still for the sitting; the souls of the later speakers are in the process of significant transformation, are, in effect, in Purgatory. Prufrock, Gerontion, and the "I" of "Lady" survey the circumstances, internal and external, which have made them what they are. Pericles, Simeon, and the Magus do likewise, but the attitudes they now take are tentative and characteristic of a stage in their spiritual progress; they contain at least a potentiality for movement absent in the earlier work. Furthermore, our attention is called more briefly to the *person* who progresses, and more fully to the nature of the progress. *The Waste Land* had already begun this tendency; *Ash Wednesday* continues it; and in *Four Quartets* the journey is almost completely depersonalized. The stages of the journey are revealed by a persona largely detached from his revelation; the stages are not stages in *a* progress of someone, but stages in the progress: the poem memorializes moments of transformation, moments of change, in virtual isolation from any person who experiences them. From the personal experience of Prufrock and Gerontion we have shifted at last to abstract experience, to the moving points around the still center of the poem or the static journey, from the *Inferno* through the *Purgatorio* to the *Paradiso*.

The validity of these observations is not reduced by the fact that the early poems vary in the degree to which their personae are circumstantially identified. Only a few personae in the early volumes are so clearly delineated as Prufrock, and these early poems can easily be divided into two kinds—those that pose a persona who talks mainly about his own situation, and those that pose a persona who talks mainly about the state of the world outside him. The personae of "Preludes," "Rhapsody on a Windy Night," and of most of Eliot's "metaphysical" poems survey the world in which they live mainly by watching the progress or lack of it in a world external to the speaker. Nevertheless, any evaluation of the world functions also as an evaluation of oneself. In "Rhapsody" the "I" is clearly implicated in the pointlessness he has described. And in other poems the poet's personae, though anonymous, are usually implicated less directly; they stand for the modern questing soul, looking upon the disorder of the world and involved in that disorder along with all other people. As a human being, the persona cannot merely observe the world; he must also evaluate it and lament it.

For observation, evaluation, and lamentation are the inevitable experiences of any perceptive persona. Even the more clearly individuated personae must, in the process of telling us about themselves, also tell us about their world. Their world is full of persons who have forgotten their purposes—English countesses, Mr. Silveros—or of institutions or great men whose achievements have been perverted—Chopin, Lazarus, Hamlet, Christ. The differences between Eliot's personae in the early poems are largely differences in the degree to which they are circumstantially identified in this world of corrupted purposes. When they are clearly identified, it is usually *their* corruption that the poem emphasizes as emblematic of human and modern corruption; when they mostly observe without participating, the emphasis is on the world's corruption. But no one is not implicated. Self is involved in the world's corruption, world is involved in the self's. The theme is the same, and only the point of view changes. And throughout all the poems both world and selves remain fixed in their damnations.

After 1925, however, Eliot's emphasis is less on corruption than on possible redemption. And his two points of view persist. In "Marina," "Song of Simeon," "Journey of the Magi," and *Ash Wednesday* he examines the experiences of spiritual progress from the point of view of the experiencer. In "Animula" and *Four Quartets* he examines the same experiences, but from the point of view of a more detached but by no means unimplicated persona. All these poems examine both world and self, and in the experiences central to each poem the persona is implicitly or explicitly involved. But he moves, or is about to move; his being is impermanent, suffused with what he is on the edge of being.

III

Such are the general characteristics of Eliot's personae. But how does he handle them in order to relate them intelligibly and effectively to the reader, to the poet, and to the poem? To answer the last two parts of this question modern criticism supplies an abundance of theory, but matters of point of view and tone, which largely define the relation of persona and reader, have rarely been adequately analyzed. All poetry is a kind of speech; insofar as it is poetry, it is all one kind of speech; but it draws on, even mocks, and certainly imitates, other categories of human utterance. The words of poetry are variously imitative of the sounds and meanings made by different sorts of men in different sorts of circumstances. Tone is the catchall word we use to describe this aspect of poetry, and it is the tones of his discourse which mainly define the relation of a persona to his reader.

What does tone tell us, and how? It tells us what kind of man the speaker is generally, and it lets us see from time to time some of his specific feelings; it further tells us the kind of audience he is addressing, and his purpose in addressing them. To a large extent, poetic tone is conveyed through the audience's detection of certain conventional rhetorical patterns of speech, which make clear either the nature of the speaker himself and his various mental and emotional phases, or the nature of his audience. These conventional rhetorical patterns of speech are themselves analyzable into patterns of sound and meaning—into, first, a diction, syntax, sentence structure, appropriate to, say, casual conversation and not oratorical address; and second, into intricate patterns of pitch, volume, and tempo, the general harmonics of which may be appropriate to lyrical, elegiac, or other kinds of utterance.

Whatever the neural justifications for these conventions of sound, we distinguish even in our silent reading of poetry between sounds of one order and sounds of another. A good reader of verse can, by the skillful manipulation of the musical dynamics of his voice, make even a reading of nonsense syllables dramatic. But in most writing the variations of tone lie in our understanding the melodic force of specific words, phrases, and syntaxes, and, even more, of their intricate combinations. We grasp their melodic force because we have heard them before, or something so close to them that they have a familiar ring. We thus accept writing as not only composed of devices of wit, imagery, plot, and other intellectually assimilable elements, but as also including sound and even as relying for much of its effect on our knowledge of conventional correlations between the sound-patterns of speech and various human situations. The sound-patterns themselves are conventional, peculiar to language, age, and culture; the various human situations are similarly restricted to those conventionally recognized as possible or typical in any society; and the correlations between them are also imposed on a poet by the poetic and social traditions of his contemporaries.

During any day spent in the company of people, one hears an almost infinite variety of tones; and the tones of any good poem of a few pages' length are hardly less various. Poetic personae characteristically use different tones to convey different emotions—fear, horror, love, pity, anger—and to convey these emotions with a thousand variations in shading; or they mix these emotions with each other—love mixed with anger, pity mixed with love, resentment mixed with pity, and infinite others. At the same time, personae traditionally take up, even in the same poem, different relationships with their audiences, now cajoling them in friendly fashion, now warning them on the basis of superior perception, now commanding them with authority, now chatting with them, now berating them, mocking them, scorning them, ignoring them, now disposing of them with gentle superiority. Indeed, any long poem, composed throughout in a consistent verse form, must necessarily vary not only the emotions of the persona but also the attitudes of the persona toward whomever he addresses, in order to avoid dullness.

Throughout most English poetry these changes in tone have been conveyed largely by musical means—by the management of pitch, volume, tempo, within a continuing scheme of versification. Many modern poets continue this practice, and all do to a certain extent, but several modern poets—notably Eliot—frequently alter the verse form along with the change in tone. *The Waste Land* is certainly the most stunning example of this. Instead of writing the whole poem in blank verse, or even in his own kind of liberated blank verse, Eliot uses a variety of metres and forms, which constantly break in upon one another with violent irruptions of tone. On the other hand, his changes in verse are, in a sense, secondary to the changes in tone which they support. And other modern poets have made frequent use of the poem that, without disturbing the metrical formula of the verse, still wrests the persona from one point of view to another—or, differently interpreted, juxtaposes two very different personae who speak in tones that clash. Yeats in particular does this in the refrains of some of his later poems, and his device has been widely imitated.

But the structure of Yeats's refrain poems is quite revolutionary and in its arrangement of tones differs even from the structure of Eliot's juxtapositional poetry. In some at least of Yeats's late poems the structural principle is quite Hegelian: two conflicting personae, or attitudes, or tones, are juxtaposed—and dropped! The reader must grasp the whole poem that emerges from their confrontation. This is a technique reminiscent of satire, but one hardly ever used in other poetry; it is only dimly anticipated by such works as *The Canterbury Tales* and is common among English poems only in certain ballads. It is not the technique of Eliot, whose poetry in this respect as in many others follows a traditional course. For in Eliot's work there is always one dominant tone to which the persona consistently returns.

The tone which dominates most of his poems is that of the progressing or defeated quester reviewing his experience for the benefit of an almost casual audience. From "Prufrock" to *Four Quartets* the dominant tone is a conversational tone. The variations, to be sure, have an almost incredible range, and they are largely responsible for the obscurity with which Eliot is so often charged; the verse changes, and transitions are omitted in this poetry of juxtaposition. But even in *The Waste Land* the persona returns from his wanderings among other speech patterns to resume the tone of casual (and usually gloomy) reminiscence:

> April is the cruellest month, breeding
> Lilacs over the dead land, mixing
> Memory and desire . . .
>
> Under the brown fog of a winter dawn,
> A crowd flowed over London bridge, so many,
> I had not thought death had undone so many.
>
> The hot water at ten.
> And if it rains, a closed car at four.
> And we shall play a game of chess . . .
>
> A rat crept softly through the vegetation
> Dragging its slimy belly on the bank . . .
>
> I Tiresias, old man with wrinkled dugs
> Perceived the scene, and foretold the rest—
> I too awaited the expected guest.

Phlebas the Phoenician, a fortnight dead,
Forgot the cry of gulls, and the deep sea swell
And the profit and loss.

Who is the third who walks always beside you?

I have heard the key
Turn in the door and turn once only

I sat upon the shore
Fishing, with the arid plain behind me

These tones are not the same by any means, but in each passage the diction is that of a smooth and easy English. They are supplemented by many passages of actual conversation—some intense, some merely animated, but phrased mostly in the language of common conversation. Indeed, if the poem is at all unsuccessful, it may be partly because, skillfully as most of the tones are assimilated to the basic one, a few of them remain not totally assimilated, notably the cry to Stetson, the gnomic laments of the Rhine-maidens, the Hindu mutters, and the excessive allusiveness in the last few lines. All of these, at least to the ear of this reader, are insufficiently harmonized with the tone of the rest of the poem, a tone that, like all of Eliot, is basically, but not continuously, conversational.

Within his basic conversational tone the speaker of *The Waste Land* ranges widely. Most frequently, as the above passages indicate, his tone is serious, if not somber. But he is occasionally capable of other feelings. At his vision of the affair between the typist and the clerk, the persona shows an ironic amusement that includes his vision of himself. There is wit in the presentation, too, of Madame Sosostris, of Lil, and of Sweeney and Mrs. Porter. And an occasional intensity rises above the conversational in the reminiscences of the protagonist's relationships with the Hyacinth girl, with Stetson, and with the Thunder.

In fact, the persona changes so much that his unity constantly verges on incoherence. Sometimes within one role he changes tone; sometimes his change of tone signalizes also a change of person: he becomes Ferdinand or the Fisher King or the modern husband. And these quick changes raise the question of the relationship between changes of tone and changes of persona. To a degree, all of us become different persons when we change our moods and the tones that go with them; our emotions as well as our social positions are roles, masks, that we take up and discard. At every moment we play different parts, and the changing tones in our words reflect the most minute changes in our attitudes. The more extreme these changes, the less coherent is our own unity; but extreme changes may also result in an increase of scope. The man or the persona capable of moving among widely different roles demonstrates the rich multiplicity of human possibility, provided he still somehow remains single. The singleness of Eliot's persona in *The Waste Land* is sometimes doubtful, but he consistently returns to his role of quester recounting in a casual but often intense English the phases of his perception.

This easy conversational tone persists, too, throughout the poems in which the "I" is more observer than participant. The diction and tone of "Preludes" are dryly conversational, as are those of "Rhapsody" and the other minor poems of Eliot's first volume. His "metaphysical" poems continue witty and casual in their tone, even though they at times—as at the end of "Sweeney among the Nightingales"—attain a greater elevation. *Ash Wednesday* adapts Eliot's usual tone to the purposes of prayer, confession, supplication, and thanksgiving, but the manner is still easy. And in *Four Quartets* virtually all the varying tones are adapted, with a skill superior even to that employed in *The Waste Land*, to the basic tone of a man talking to various auditors—to a few friends, to God, and perhaps to himself.[1] In *Quartets* the few lines that stand out as not quite right are mainly lapses in tone; the author has not fully assimilated these tones to his basic one. The "Garlic and sapphires" passage is notably deficient in this respect: the tone of a gnomic riddle is out of place. So are such lines as

> I do not know much about gods . . .

or

> I sometimes wonder if that is what Krishna
> meant . . .

In the first the pose of intellectual innocence fails to convince, and the casual phrasing of the second cannot, for the ordinary reader even of Eliot, contain the word Krishna without absurdity. In each case the attempted variation of the conversational tone has failed to connect suitably with the picture of the persona given by the rest of the poem.

In summary, then, we can say that one principal unifying force in Eliot's poetry is the tone that underlies each poem, and the tone in turn defines the level at which the persona meets the reader. As a rule, Eliot holds his persona firmly to a conversational level, but because of this firm base can allow him to explore an assortment of other audience-defining tones—prophecy, lyric apostrophe, formal lamentation—so long as he always returns to his base. The result is a richness and variety of tone rare in any nondramatic verse and, indeed, seldom achieved in traditional drama. In his plays Eliot has been held too closely to a one- or two-tone drama, with the consequence that the rich textures of his verse, founded on the freedom to range almost at will among tones, are lost to him on the stage. Among his longer poems only *The Hollow Men* has a base not that of conversational language, in consequence of which perhaps its texture is thinner than that of his more successful works, and its almost unrelieved dreariness more a triumph of wit than of poetry.

The conversational tone of most of Eliot's work invites the reader to accept the persona in a more or less equal relationship. The persona does not speak down to the reader—even in *Four Quartets* he addresses the reader as a friend except in a few falsely humble, rather patronizing lines that tend to weaken the equal relationship. But while the conversational base defines the rapport between reader and persona, within the conversational tone the persona reveals a pattern of emotional response appropriate to his role as questing man. The talk of *The Waste Land* reflects in turn the speaker's aspiration and despair, his capacity for ecstasy and humor, his union of sense and sensibility which makes him a representative man. The tones reveal the man, his cosmic situation, and his relation to the reader; it might even more accurately be said that a definition of each of these includes a definition of the others. The persona is involved in the same world as the reader; as his world defines his own role, his own self, so it defines both the reader's pattern of responses and his involvement with all other men in a human world. In fact, the deliberate reproduction of the tones of casual speech, of what Wordsworth called "the real language of men in a state of vivid sensation," has been felt in our century and the last to signify the commonalty of all human experience. Yet because in Eliot there exists no real discontinuity between the self and its cosmic situation, the reader's identification with the persona is doubtfully pure. Reader and persona are emblems of each other. The poet and the reader share the persona's situation—his traffic among tones, his quest. As the following pages will show, however, they share with each other more than the persona shares with them. The "hypocrite lecteur" is assuredly the persona's "semblable," but he is also more fully the poet's.

IV

In his criticism Eliot has repeatedly discussed the relation between the poet and his personae. He has been especially concerned to distinguish between the poet's emotions and the emotions of the characters he presents. "No artist," he writes, "produces great art by a deliberate attempt to express his personality." [*SE*, 96] And again: "Poetry is not a turning loose of emotion . . . it is not the expression of personality." [*SE*, 10] Emotion—even the poet's emotion—has its place in a poem, but it is not *directly* expressed. "What every poet starts from is his own emotions" [*SE*, 117], but:

> It is not in his personal emotions, the emotions provoked by particular events in his life, that the poet is in any way remarkable or interesting. His particular emotions may be simple, or crude, or flat. The emotion in his poetry will be a very complex thing, but not with the complexity of the emotions of people who have very complex or unusual emotions in life. [*SE*, 10]

The process by which the artist's emotions become poetry is subtle and indirect:

> It is suggested, then, that a dramatic poet cannot create characters of the greatest intensity of life unless his personages, in their reciprocal actions and behaviour in their story, are somehow dramatizing, but in no obvious form, an action or struggle for harmony in the soul of the poet. [*SE*, 172–173]

The soul of the poet, and not merely his emotion, is the source of the struggle, and of the harmony. The soul presumably includes the entire psychic life, and between its dynamics and the events of the poem a subtle correlation exists. We have to remember, however, that it is a correlation between totalities, a transformation of the psychic life into the very different terms of art, not merely a point-by-point translation into discrete linguistic symbols. Goethe's Mephistopheles, for example, is unsatisfactory because he "embodies a philosophy. A creation of art should not do that: he should *replace* the philosophy." [*SW*, 66] Dante, on the other hand, "has succeeded in dealing with his philosophy, not as a theory . . . or as his own comment or reflection, but in terms of something *perceived.*" [*SW*, 170–171]

Is the method of *Faust* really different in kind from the method of *The Divine Comedy,* or does the latter simply excel in the degree to which it translates the psychic life into symbolic wholes rather than into allegorical pieces? Where does literature cease to be literature and become merely imaginative language? As one can see even from his apparently unfair but significant comparison of the character Mephistopheles with the whole of *The Divine Comedy,* Eliot's answer appears to depend on the context in which the poetic elements figure. Not symbols so much as how they function together is his main criterion for judging poetry. Even in the individual sections of a work Eliot is more concerned with the concord between elements than with the immediate representational function of each element. Thus, his idea of the objective correlative is phrased in terms that reveal his contextual point of view:

> The only way of expressing emotion in the form of art is by finding an 'objective correlative'; in other words, a set of objects, a situation, a chain of events which shall be the formula of that *particular* emotion; such that when the external facts, which must terminate in sensory experience, are given, the emotion is immediately evoked. [*SE*, 124–125]

Not an object, but a *set* of objects; not an event, but a *chain* of events. Every unit in the poem, analyzable into specific images, words, and sounds, has meaning *as a whole.* The specific elements do not translate immediately into meanings and then add up into larger meanings. They work together *in the poem* and translate as wholes into meanings. Even though we must grasp the meanings of individual words and sounds, we instantly, as it were, send those meanings back into the poem until they have taken their place in larger units that are then retranslated back to us as wholes.

If this is true for the small units, it is also true for the larger units, and ultimately for the whole poem. Behind the whole poem lies the fundamental emotion or feeling or complex of feeling—the psychic structure—of which the poem is a symbolic realization. All the conventions and devices of poetry—the plot, the characters, the imagery, the verse form—exist to be manipulated in such a way as to provide in their totality the "formula" of the poet's feeling. So in the metaphysical poets a "telescoping of images and multiplied associations" is used because the poets "were, at best, engaged in the task of trying to find the verbal equivalent for states of mind and feeling." [*SE*, 243, 248] States of mind and feeling are larger than emotions. And, as Eliot says, looking into the heart "is not looking deep enough. . . . One must look into the cerebral cortex, the nervous system, and the digestive tracts." [*SE*, 250] In order to express the whole man, not merely his emotions, the poet's mind must be "constantly amalgamating disparate experience." [*SE*, 247] His "perceptions," like those of any "really appreciative mind," do not "accumulate as a mass, but form themselves as a structure." [*SW*, 15] The various elements in verse must be used in drama

> to get upon the stage [a] precise statement of life which is at the same time a point of view, a world —a world which the author's mind has subjected to a complete process of simplification. [*SW*, 68]

And this is possible because

> To create a form is not merely to invent a shape, a rhyme or rhythm. It is also the realization of the

> whole appropriate content of this rhyme or rhythm. The sonnet of Shakespeare is not merely such and such a pattern, but a precise way of thinking and feeling. [*SW*, 63]

In this process the whole life of the author is transfused into the work:

> The creation of a work of art, we will say the creation of a character in a drama, consists in the transfusion of the personality, or, in a deeper sense, the life, of the author into the character. This is a very different matter from the orthodox creation in one's own image. [*SE*, 137]

To support his position Eliot quotes Remy de Gourmont's description of Flaubert:

> Flaubert incorporait toute sa sensibilité à ses oeuvres. . . . Hors de ses livres, où il se transvasait goutte à gouette [*sic*], jusqu'à la lie, Flaubert est fort peu intéressant. [*SE*, 193]

And Eliot adds that we can say of certain poets that they, too, "*se transvasaient goutte à gouette*" [*sic*]. Since the process is one of transfusion and not of direct expression, "A poet can express his feelings as fully through a dramatic, as through a lyrical form"; and, consequently, "for a poet with dramatic gifts, a situation quite remote from his personal experience may release the strongest emotion." [*SE*, 290]

The poet, then, is to be thought of as a whole man, directing his whole self, with all its ideas, prejudices, emotions, and attitudes, toward one subject or problem after another in one poem after another. The whole self is one whole, and the whole poem is another; and the poem is the objective correlative, the poetic equivalent, of the whole man. It is his "personality" that does, in fact, confer a unity on the poem and, indeed, on the whole body of a poet's work:

> The whole of Shakespeare's work is *one* poem. . . . A man might, hypothetically, compose any number of fine passages or even of whole poems

> which would each give satisfaction, and yet not be a great poet, unless we felt them to be united by one significant, consistent, and developing personality. [*SE*, 179]

A poet's work is usually distinguished by a "tone," or series of tones, which is peculiar to him:

> Every writer who has written any blank verse worth saving has produced particular tones which his verse and no other's is capable of rendering. . . . Shakespeare is 'universal' because he has more of these tones than any one else; but they are all out of the one man . . . . [*SE*, 101]

Every poet thus has his own tonality, which is to be associated with a unique way of looking at life. As Eliot says of Ford's verse,

> Even in so late and so decayed a drama as that of Ford, the framework of emotions and morals of the time is only the vehicle for statements of feeling which are unique and imperishable: Ford's and Ford's only. [*SE*, 189]

And he says in the same essay that an involved style "should follow the involutions of a mode of perceiving, registering, and digesting impressions which is also involved." [*SE*, 187] Since Massinger's feelings and ideas are conventional and derivative, so ultimately is his verse. "Marlowe's and Jonson's comedies," on the other hand,

> were a view of life; they were, as great literature is, the transformation of a personality into a personal work of art, their lifetime's work, long or short. Massinger is not simply a smaller personality: his personality hardly exists. [*SE*, 192]

Of Jonson's drama he says elsewhere: "what holds the play together is a unity of inspiration that radiates into plots and personages alike." [*SE*, 134] And of Shakespeare:

> It has been said that Shakespeare lacks unity; it might, I think, be said equally well that it is

> Shakespeare chiefly that *is* the unity . . . [*SE*, 119]

Heywood's work is another matter: "to inform the verse there is no vision, none of the artist's power to give undefinable unity to the most various material." [*SE*, 152] In his contemporaries "there is at least some inchoate pattern; there is, as it would often be called, personality." [*SE*, 153]

By finding, in both the detail and design of a work, the appropriate correlative of the poet's feeling (his soul, his ideas, his attitudes, his whole self), the poet will transfuse himself into his poems and so confer on it the unity of his own personality. On one level, then, the poet's aim is to make a total verbal equivalent for his total feeling; in effect, one purpose of the poet in writing *is* to express his personality. But this is personality in the largest sense, and its expression in the poem is less an aim than an inevitable product. Eliot believes the poet has other, more immediate purposes in composing any poem. These purposes appear to have little to do with the reader:

> The poet does not aim to excite—that is not even a test of his success—but to set something down; the state of the reader is merely that reader's particular mode of perceiving what the poet has caught in words. [*SW*, 170]

But what has the poet caught in words besides his own personality? Again Eliot writes:

> The emotion of art is impersonal. And the poet cannot reach this impersonality without surrendering himself wholly to the work to be done. [*SE*, 11]

But what is the work to be done? It is evidently not the expression of one's own emotion; this gets done, but it should not be the poet's intention to do it. The work to be done, according to Eliot, is the presentation of a "statement" or a "vision" of life.

A "vision of life" sounds very much like a "personality." The former is inevitably dependent on the latter, or even a part of it. But they are, more accurately, two sides of the same coin and not the same side. A poem is a formulation of the poet's sense of the world in which he lives. Such a formulation must reflect the psychic structure of the poet, but so, to one degree or another, does all writing. The writer's personality is merely implicit in poems as in other written work. If a writer discusses his own personality *in* his writing, we should presumably interpret this first as significant for our understanding of his view of life; but our sense of his total personality, of the form of his mind, will be extractable rather from the form and the manner of the discussion than from anything we are explicitly told.

For it is in the choice and arrangement of his materials, not in his explicit statements, that the poet most fully reveals himself. Affirmations and disavowals that the persona makes more or less directly, serve only to clarify the poet's attitude toward life. But an attitude is not a mind; the poet's psychic life is larger than his view of life; and we understand his soul only as we understand both the view of life presented in the poem and the way in which it is presented. In any final analysis, perhaps, the two are inseparable; their interpenetration is thorough, and we cannot comprehend either the mind without knowing the view of life, or the view of life without the structure of its presentation.

But for the duration of the poem the poet's mind makes no overt intrusion. Eliot regards the poet's position as almost a passive one: he is a catalytic agent, a "finely perfected medium in which special, or very varied, feelings are at liberty to enter into new combinations." [*SE*, 7] And, consequently, "the progress of the artist is a continual self-sacrifice, a continual extinction of personality." [*SE*, 7] He does not feel the emotions of his personae, though he may at some time have felt emotions like them. In fact,

> the more perfect the artist, the more completely separate in him will be the man who suffers and the mind which creates; the more perfectly will the mind digest and transmute the passions which are its material. [*SE*, 7–8]

But although the personality of the poet should be kept out of the parts of the poem, it enters the poem as a whole. It is visible in the total form, the total style, of the completed work. The artist is freed from the necessity of having emotions and personality, at least for the time of composition, and his job is to concentrate so on the work to be done—the finding of a verbal equivalent for his feeling—that his whole experience fuses into a new thing, the poem, the work of art.

> For it is not the 'greatness,' the intensity, of the emotions, the components, but the intensity of the artistic process, the pressure, so to speak, under which the fusion takes place, that counts. [*SE*, 8]

For example, in *The Waste Land,* although the protagonist's quest is essentially the same quest as Eliot's, it is inside the poem instead of outside, and at no particular point in the poem is Eliot participating in the emotions of his personae. What we have is "an artistic conscience arranging emotions," not feeling them out loud; or "the transformation of a personality into a personal work of art, [one's] lifetime's work, long or short." [*SE*, 187, 192] Of the sudden transitions and juxtapositions of modern poetry Eliot has said: "Whether the transition is cogent or not, is merely a question of whether the mind is *serré* or *delié,* whether the whole personality is involved." [*SE*, 446]

Thus, neither the persona nor his statements are to be interpreted as directly representative of the poet and his psychic life. Taken outside the poem, the poem's statements of belief might be shared by the poet; but as the poem stands, the statements are within it, and the total beliefs that the poem expresses are inseparable from the form that contains them, and are modified by that form, and the form that contains and modifies the beliefs reflects as a whole the total personality of the poet, and, more importantly, asserts the poet's total view of life.

Not only, then, is Eliot the poet to be considered as separate from characters like Prufrock and Gerontion and Tiresias, but he is also distinct from the speakers of such poems as "Preludes," *Ash Wednesday*, and *Four Quartets*. In every poem certain situations, certain sets of objects, certain chains of events, as well as the characters themselves and the sounds and meanings of the words, the lines, the sections—all work together to form a whole pattern whose immediate implication to a sensitive reader is a formulation of a view of life, and whose further implication, deeper but more incidental to the apparent purposes of the poet, lies in the reflection of the poet's whole personality. Even the direct statements of *Four Quartets* and *Ash Wednesday* have a double function: they must be understood as units of meaning, but, once understood (whether or not they are assented to), they must be sent back into the current of the poem so that the reader will grasp their context, the total statement that the poetic form adumbrates.

Eliot tells us, in his early essay on "Dante":

> The aim of the poet is to state a vision, and no vision of life can be complete which does not include the articulate formulation of life which human minds make. [*SW*, 170]

The vision *includes* the formulation by particular personae, but it is larger; it is itself a larger formulation in nonexplicit, in poetic, form. The ritual performers, the conversational tones, are merely the result of Eliot's choice, largely deliberate, among possible techniques for presenting his view of reality. That he chooses these techniques tells us much about his view of reality and about his own mental being. The various poetic materials reflect his conscious poetic intelligence as well as the structure of his personality. But the poem is the thing, and in the poem the statement of belief is presented, not confessed; the feelings of the speaker are depicted, not shared; and the persona is a point of view *in* the poem, not the point of view of the poet.

Thus, although the reader may be inveigled into reading a poem by his tentative identification with its persona, he must, if he is to grasp the poem, encounter the poet elsewhere, at a point where reader and poet together can see the poem as a whole. Everything in the poem must be clarified by reference to the world outside the poem, but this system of repeated reference is a technique of the poem, not a series of valid truths. Each denotating element, including the persona, must take its meaning from the world that is the poem. And just as Mephistopheles should not embody a philosophy but, like *The Divine Comedy*, replace it, so Prufrock and Gerontion and the "I" of *Four Quartets* are incomplete if we take their message to be what they more or less tell us it is. Not what the personae say, nor what they embody, but what the poem *is*, is the point. Instead of presenting an instance of human experience, the poem provides an experience, is, in its role of artifact undergone, an experience itself. Poet and reader *have* the experience together; and it is in the having of it—not in the seeing of it, as in Browning, nor in the pretending to have someone else's, as in the Romantics—that poet and reader coincide. The experience is neither simulated nor observed, though both simulation and observation may enter into it as functions of the persona; but the experience is immediate and actual.

But why is the experience of reading a poem valuable? Immediately, perhaps, because its substance is the world we compose, and the poem is a re-creation of the pattern of our own life. Ultimately, perhaps, because poems are instances of one mode of comprehending meaning, and hence one mode of making meaning; thus, while to use the mode is valuable, to contemplate it in its instances is to penetrate not merely the patterns of our social existence, but also the pattern of experience which underlies the artistic formulation of that social existence. In experiencing the poem, in short, we experience art as well as art's vision of life. Possibly, this is why critics enjoy modern poetry more than other people do; critics come to the poem with their minds already full of poetic theory. And an Eliotan poem gives them not only a vision of life but an instance of art, an instance that the poet deliberately arranges to give, as one of his most important aims in writing his poems. To understand a poem by Eliot we must leave the persona and grasp the poem at the level at which it asserts both the world and itself, and, through itself, the value of artistic expression—the value of singing.

3

Yeats: The Tradition of Myself

ANY GENERALIZATION about the nature of modern poetry inevitably runs up against the intransigeant poetry of Yeats, and at that point often requires modification. This is true for several reasons, mainly perhaps because the poetry of Yeats is so many things and resists general statements about it as a whole, but also because in the process of "modernizing" himself Yeats carried into his mature poetry so much of the later nineteenth-century poetic paraphernalia that are not modern. His choice of poems for *The Oxford Book of Modern Verse, 1892–1935* (New York, 1936) is revealing. The poets to whom he gives the greatest space do not belong to the school of Eliot and Pound, nor to the later group of Auden, Day Lewis, MacNeice, and Spender. The bulk of the book is given over to writers of the nineties or of later decades who accept and make use of a very unmodern mythology of dreams, desires, and passionate expressions of passionate longings. The poets are in love with Death, with Love, with their own Passionate Experience, and they are concerned to state their particular emotions. In such roles as those of lover, sage, sensualist, they tell the reader how they feel. There is no satire: poems descriptive of people or of the world aim at the expression of pathos or indignation, and the statement of emotion is decorated with rhyme and meter in order to make it a poem. Of the ninety-seven poets included in the volume, perhaps a dozen would be considered "modern" by an Eliot or a Pound. In fact, taken as a whole, Yeats's selection of modern verse exhibits qualities of Victorian and decadent poetry against which several prominent modern poets had, by 1935, been struggling for more than twenty years.

The fact is indicative. However formal his own poetry became, Yeats himself remained more sympathetic to a poetry that dealt with violent, barely controllable passions than to the "grey, cold, dry" art of Eliot. Eliot's impersonal recorder is not a persona that appeals to Yeats. The "I" of Yeats is usually at the center of the stage, passionate, choosing, involved in the action; just as the hero of nineteenth-century English poetry is usually the poet and is dramatized (or at least talked about) throughout the poem. Yeats alters the pattern he inherited, but his alteration is not that of Eliot. Instead of the blurred, shadowy, withdrawn personae whose observations, selected and arranged, are an objective correlative of the poet's feeling, Yeats's "I" becomes through his poetry less and less remote, less and less withheld; but it is cut up into fragments, and the fragmentation is quite as stylized as the impersonality of Eliot, and in effect just as impersonal.

Ezra Pound, speaking of *The Cantos*, tells us that the poem can probably be thought of best as dividing its material into "the permanent, the recurrent, the casual." [*Letters*, 239] Such a division is useful also for understanding the world of Yeats. For him the soul and its passion are *permanent*, going through life after life; the particular setting in which passion takes place is *casual*, and so are all the trivial details of our daily lives and our decaying civilizations; but the conflict between the trivial and the passionate, between the temporary and the eternal, and the different forms that the conflict takes, are *recurrent*. "My instructors identify consciousness with conflict," he tells us in *A Vision*. [p. 214] This conflict is central to his poetry, but the handling of the conflict varies with the stages of his development into a mature poet.

The recurrent conflict between the permanent and the casual is not an unusual subject for poetry. Its use as a favorite theme in English literature can be pointed out as early as the medieval morality plays, and Eliot's use of it has already been noted. In particular, a great deal of Victorian energy was spent in the production of poems that associated the moral difficulties of poets with those of other passionate men of other ages who were also in conflict with their worlds. Yeats's involvement in the theme is, in fact, typical for a poet of his time; only his pursuit of it for fifty-odd years through a variety of poetic forms and through the elaboration of a fantastic pseudophilosophic schematization is remarkable.

Yeats's treatment of this theme falls into two main categories. The early poems, for the most part, deal with the conflict in vague, general, and "poetical" terms. The heavenly side of the opposition is usually presented through characters who are, in the best Romantic tradition, poetic exaggerations of the aspirations of the poet: Oisin, Aengus, Forgael. The trivial daily world from which the poet wishes to escape is largely made up either of natural phenomena (clouds, autumn, beasts, the sea, winds) around which gather gloomy and dreamy associations, or of those supernatural beings whose immemorial business is malice. Both groups, while they represent forces antagonistic to passion, are forcefully presented, but they seem, in the fashion of other Victorian poetry, too little distinct from the forces that support passion. The dimensions of both passion and antipassion are identical, and the battle between them is consequently vague.

But the technique to which Yeats came in his later days was very different, and the change consisted not in any important modification of the basic conflict, but rather in making both sides of the opposition more concrete and precise. The exaggerated passion of the early "I" becomes either any of a number of personae whose social and geographical worlds are precisely located by the poet, or Yeats himself in one or more of his roles: poet, householder, father, old man, Irish public figure, and so on. The vague and gloomy, but suggestive, evil of the early poems is located more distinctly in the Irish mob or Yeats's political or literary opponents, or, more poignantly, is symbolized by decrepitude of body or low social position. The increasing vividness of the portrayal of the forces opposed to passion gives the conflict dramatic power. An Oisin or a Forgael, cut off as he is in his dream-world from the limitations of time and space, can have no convincing trouble in discovering the eternal; but when lecherous old Irish men and women can discover it, their struggle has drama, and the drama has point.

Accordingly, whereas the early poems show the poet posing as a legendary hero or as lover, sage, or other passionate man, the later poetry presents a persona (himself or another) who is more involved in the petty events of the world and whose achievement of a satisfactory relationship with the eternal is, consequently, so much more praiseworthy. The pose of the early poems is not gone: the character of Yeats, as it appears in these later poems, is always posing. He fancies himself as a sage, a lover, an Irish legend, as "in on" the secrets of the dead and the eternally living, but there is, throughout, an element of self-mockery: an exaggeration of his bodily infirmities, an emphasis on his vanity and other foibles, a continual calling of attention to his physical and mental shortcomings. In effect, the character of Yeats constantly divides into the poser and the mocker, into the man of vision and the sightless eye sockets, into the absurd old madman ragged on a heath and the great man, unaccountably convincing, who says, "Ay, every inch a king!" The whole man, Yeats or anyone living, who sees into the eternal is necessarily both sage and fool, and where the discrepancy is most strongly shown, the drama should be most effective.

II

In accordance with the best traditions of Romantic and Victorian poetry, Yeats began, he tells us, as a boy

> to play at being a sage, a magician or a poet. I had many idols, and as I climbed along the narrow ledge I was now Manfred on his glacier, and now Prince Athanase with his solitary lamp, but I soon chose Alastor for my chief of men and longed to share his melancholy, and maybe at last to disappear from everybody's sight as he disappeared drifting in a boat along some slow-moving river between great trees. [*Auto,* 39]

Throughout his childhood Yeats saw himself in one role after another, and the habit, he thinks, was a good one:

> I was about to learn that if a man is to write lyric poetry he must be shaped by nature and art to some one out of half a dozen traditional poses, and be lover or saint, sage or sensualist, or mere mocker of all life . . . [*Auto,* 53]

Since Yeats's use of himself as a persona is closely connected with his view of these traditional poses, it is useful to review briefly the nineteenth-century background of the poetic pose, and to see how Yeats used it in his own way.

In the poetry of the great Romantics the poet stands, as never before, at the center of the world and at the center of his poems. To an extent unknown in earlier verse, the poet became a *person* in his own writing, a self with a unique and particular history. This poetic development represents only part of a general philosophical movement that regarded the self as the center, and often as the creator, of all reality. We see the results of this development throughout the poetry of the nineteenth century. The lyric becomes less and less anonymous, more and more personal, concerned not so much with the graceful expression of commonplaces or with the skillful expression of subtle but impersonal thought as with the sincere expression of ideas or feelings that belong, in a quite personal way, to the poet himself. The drama is often a lyrical drama, and the narrative poem frequently presents heroes who function as idealized versions of their creators.

In the last century and a half we have become accustomed to find the poet overtly present in his poems, exhibiting his personality in all its strength and variety. But to the early nineteenth-century poet the presentation of himself in his own poem, not as a minor character nor as an almost anonymous focus for words and events, but as the generously delineated center of the action, was an unusual and challenging poetic technique. It involved, inevitably, a selection of details, and the characteristic nineteenth-century selection was self-flattering in the extreme. The poet as hero was a hero indeed: sensitive to the beauty of nature, sympathetic with human suffering, divested of all the trivial qualities that belong to persons in everyday life, he made no gestures that were not strong or graceful, spoke no words that were unimpassioned, participated in no actions that were not in some way grand or noble. Even his weaknesses, even his vices, had a certain attractiveness. The picture of himself which the Romantic poet presented, made up as it was of an amalgam of qualities drawn from various traditional heroic figures —knight, courtier, prophet, magician, and others—was far from an accurate reproduction; it was clearly a pose.

We cannot penetrate very far into nineteenth-century verse before we find the personae and characters posing, posturing, attitudinizing. Shelley, Byron, Tennyson, Whitman, Swinburne, are only a few of the poets who, faced with the problem of using themselves, or selves like themselves, in their poems, developed gestures and attitudes that seemed, in and out of poetry, to suit the character of the "Poet." This pose is clearly an artificial self, at least in part. But, placed in the poem, it serves the nineteenth-century poet as subject, as an "I" around which the world revolves. It stands for the poet, who may even try in his daily life to imitate it.

But any pose we assume, so long as it remains a pose and does not become part of what we treat without thinking as our more immediate selves, is outside of us, is in effect a depicted thing, an object rather than a subject. If we contemplate it *as* a pose, it is a third-person thing, like a part of our clothing, like an actual mask. In the nineteenth century most poets assume the pose without such contemplation; as it appears in poems, the pose is meant to stand for the poet without significant qualification. But a few poets stand aside from their poses and regard them with at least partial detachment and even mockery.

Among the English Romantic poets mockery came most easily to Byron. The heroes of his narrative poems experience the usual exalted emotions of Romantic poetry and appear to represent the sensibilities of their creator. But Byron was also aware of a faint absurdity in the attitudes struck by his heroes and personae, and in *Don Juan* he continually mocks his own poses along with those of his hero. He frequently uses apostrophes to nature and to man, so fashionable in the serious poetry of the day, merely to hold up his narrative at a point of suspense or as ironic contrast to the vivid sexuality of his story. Furthermore, the poem is full of references to details of life which do not ordinarily find their way into heroic poems; indeed, at its deepest level the poem is a brutal satire on the manners of fashionable society and an exposure of the lusts that underlie its pretended aspirations. Behind every institution that modern society holds sacred Byron shows us either the absurdity or the corruption. But the satire seems almost accidental; the persona never ceases to pose. In the midst of serious assertions he continually breaks off to assure the reader that he, at least, unlike members of modern hypocritical society, does not take his postures too seriously, but this assurance is in itself a very serious posture and one which the persona does take seriously. In the following stanzas, for example, notice the succession of attitudes:

> Some kinder casuists are pleased to say,
> In nameless print—that I have no devotion;
> But set those persons down with me to pray,
> And you shall see who has the properest notion
> Of getting into heaven the shortest way;
> My altars are the mountains and the ocean,
> Earth, air, stars,—all that springs from the great Whole,
> Who hath produced, and will receive the soul.
>
> Sweet hour of twilight!—in the solitude
> Of the pine forest, and the silent shore
> Which bounds Ravenna's immemorial wood,
> Rooted where once the Adrian wave flow'd o'er,
> To where the last Caesarean fortress stood,
> Evergreen forest! which Boccaccio's lore
> And Dryden's lay made haunted ground to me,
> How have I loved the twilight hour and thee!
>
> . . . .
>
> Soft hour! which wakes the wish and melts the heart
> Of those who sail the seas, on the first day
> When they from their sweet friends are torn apart;
> Or fills with love the pilgrim on his way
> As the far bell of vesper makes him start,
> Seeming to weep the dying day's decay;
> Is this a fancy which our reason scorns?
> Ah! surely nothing dies but something mourns!
>
> When Nero perish'd by the justest doom
> Which ever the destroyer yet destroy'd,
> Amidst the roar of liberated Rome,

Of nations freed, and the world overjoy'd,
Some hands unseen strew'd flowers upon his tomb:
Perhaps the weakness of a heart not void
Of feeling for some kindness done, when power
Had left the wretch an uncorrupted hour.

But I'm digressing; what on earth has Nero,
Or any such like sovereign buffoons,
To do with the transactions of my hero,
More than such madmen's fellow man—the moon's?
Sure my invention must be down at zero,
And I grown one of many 'wooden spoons'
Of verse (the name with which we Cantabs please
To dub the last of honours in degrees).

[Canto III, stanzas civ–cv, cviii–cx]

There is no indication that in the last, self-mocking stanza Byron means to deny the value of most of the sentiments his persona has just expressed. The mockery appears not because Byron no longer believes what he has said but because it is part of his purpose to indicate the gulf between the sublimity of noble sentiments and prosaic common sense, and also to show how dangerously near to bathos sublimity can be. But the attack is on bathos, not on sublimity, and the persona mocks himself whenever his extended apostrophes cross the line, whenever, that is to say, he is in danger of taking his pose too seriously.

The result is a sequence of attitudes—mockery breaking into seriousness, seriousness reaching toward sublimity, sublimity descending into bathos, bathos interrupted by mockery. These are all reflections of Byron's intellectual character, and the "I," consequently, never ceases to represent Byron. But the presentation of such an "I" obviously differs from the practice of most Romantic poetry in which the "I" is typically a unit of sensibility and remains a unit through the most varied experiences. Where the "I" of Wordsworth's *Prelude* reacts to all events with more or less the same alertness, intelligence, and soberness, Byron's "I" in *Don Juan* moves uncertainly between seriousness and mockery.

The self-mockery of Byron's narrator in *Don Juan*, while it had little influence on nineteenth-century poetry in England, found more interested imitators and adaptors on the Continent. And through the adaptations of the technique to German and French poetry, particularly in the work of Heine, Corbière, and Laforgue, the possibilities of ironic self-mockery were kept very much alive. Usefully so, for this diminished "I" is a technique significantly different from the usual Romantic practice of "augmentation," in which the poet's situation is associated with the more brilliant and colorful situations either of his posed self or of historical, legendary, or fictitious characters, and in which the poet-hero speaks and acts, in either lyric or narrative poem, from the depths of a bottomless passion. Instead of exaggerating his capacities and ignoring his inevitable limitations, a poem that revolves around a diminished "I" will acknowledge and even emphasize the foibles of its hero. Most nineteenth-century lyric verse of this kind either denies the values (or their possibility of attainment) of the more orthodox Romantic heroes, or asserts them in paradoxical form: the vision of evil brings with it the same ecstatic augmentations of the hero as the vision of good. For the twentieth-century lyric poet the emphasis often changes. As the self is less central in the poet's universe, his diminution need not be illusory; the hero need not be all good underneath. Yeats's emphasis is on the world, not on the self, and thus the broader view he takes of the "total situation" makes him note the value of the diminution not to the man but to the situation from which the man derives his value.

Whereas Byron moved from one pose to another, later nineteenth-century poets and critics went so far as to construct a kind of ethics on the basis of the pose. One implication of the pose is that only passionate experiences are valuable, and Pater's doctrine of exquisite moments is hardly more than a recognition of this implication, and an extension of its validity from the realm of art to the realm of ethics. According to this view, not only art but life itself should be consistently intense; not only the narrative hero or the lyric "I," but the poet himself, the actual man, should experience nothing but what is brilliant and passionate.

Beginning with this view, Oscar Wilde worked out a theory of the mask which anticipated in some respects some of the formulations of more modern poets. According to Wilde,

> what is interesting about people in good society . . . is the mask that each of them wears, not the reality that lies behind the mask. [*Essays*, 42]

The truth that Wilde is getting at, a truth reflected throughout modern literature, is that people are, in their fundamental natures, all alike; what are individual are their superficial personalities. But the mask is not merely a collection of trivial trappings that cover our common humanness; the mask is better than we are because, among "people in good society," it is the result of careful workmanship. And through the process by which we create out of ourselves an artificial self, that self is in some way liberated from the limitations of our ordinary self. In fact, the mask, as the result of so much loving care, becomes our truer self: "Man is least himself when he talks in his own person. Give him a mask, and he will tell you the truth." [*Essays*, 164]

The mask, or pose, is valuable because it is itself a work of art, and works of art are more expressive than people. The "real artist . . . [proceeds] not from feeling to form, but from form to thought and passion." [*Essays*, 175] Consequently, it is through the formal mask that we can find the truth of ourselves, as it is through the work of art that we can express or find or recognize feeling. And just as "costume is a means of displaying character without description, and of producing dramatic situations and dramatic effects"; and as rhyme is "a spiritual element of thought and passion"; [*Essays*, 32, 105] so the apparently adventitious elements of the personality which, collectively, we call the mask are in fact the bearers of metaphorical truth. The created form, in life as in art, is more valuable than the chaos it replaces.

Between the mask of Wilde and the mask of Yeats there are significant similarities. Both men thought of the mask as a constructed personality morally and artistically superior to the natural personality; and both believed that the difference between the two was analogous to the difference between art and life, between a poem and a man. For Yeats a man could attain a fuller realization of himself through art instead of through life; the poem could be the means of remolding the world somewhat nearer to the heart's austere desire. He accordingly developed a poetry that served as a realization of the man, a crystallization of the best and most fundamental part of him. At the same time, relying on conflict as the principle of his lyric presentation of the world, he saw the discrepancy between art and life, between mask and man, differently from his nineteenth-century predecessor. Although the mask is superior to the man, it cannot be presented in isolation. What the poet aspires to be can be realized in the poem, but only by emphasizing the conflict between aspiration and degradation. The contriving poet must present, for his own best expression, not only the idealized mask but also the "rag-and-bone shop" of the trivial quotidian personality out of which the mask grows and in relevance to which the mask is significant achievement. By grounding great human action in all that is most undignifyingly human, Yeats gave his conception of the noble a different and deeper turn than any ironic nineteenth-century poet dreamed of giving to his own. Under his treatment the nineteenth-century pose becomes a movable part of the poem, as Wilde saw that it must; but it was Yeats, not Wilde, who was able to realize in his own work the fullest implications of this insight.

III

The whole progress of Yeats's poetry can be construed as a development in his use of the mask; it begins mainly as the traditional Romantic pose, as the "I" of subjective experience, but as his verse matures it becomes an object to examine, a person to depict, different in identity from the poet. In his youth, as he tells us, he had

> made a new religion, almost an infallible church of poetic tradition, of a fardel of stories, and of personages, and of emotions, inseparable from their first expression, passed on from generation to generation by poets and painters with some help from philosophers and theologians. . . . I had even created a dogma: 'Because those imaginary people are created out of the deepest instinct of man, to be his measure and his norm, whatever I can imagine those mouths speaking may be the nearest I can go to truth.' [*Auto*, 71]

This dogma animates the early poetry of Yeats and, to some extent, all his work. He imagines people speaking —Indians, sad and happy shepherds, Fergus, Aengus, old pensioners, old fishermen, old foxhunters, the people of Faery, mad kings, old mothers, young women, the fiddler of Dooney, and himself as lover and poet. And all speak out of a deep knowledge of, or a passing acquaintance with, eternal values. Most of these personae are traditional heroes of poetry or folklore, but even in these early poems there are suggestions of the diminished hero—the hero whose imperfections are emphasized by the poet in order to make still more emphatic his overcoming of imperfection. So the old woman who scrubs and bakes and sweeps and blows up the fire on her knees, the mad King Goll, Moll Magee, the old fisherman and the old foxhunter, and the good-for-nothing fiddler of Dooney, must be distinguished by their frailties from the Indian or the shepherds or the heroes of Irish legend. Yeats himself, when he enters the early poems, is usually cast as poet or lover, without flaws; he is unidentified, unlocated in time and place. He is poor, he dreams, drinks ale, weaves songs, has moods, loves, and is sad; but in all this, nothing differentiates him from the hordes of passionate young men of his time who also do these things. Essentially, he does not *act*, and his communion with the eternal, like the communion of his legendary personae, is the consequence not of his moral choice but of his occupation. By virtue of *being* a poet, lover, magician, sage, he and his heroes are granted special prerogatives. In the early poems neither the diminished personae nor the vaguer augmented ones are involved in choices. Among Yeats's late poems the most dramatic and the most successful are usually those in which, in spite of all pressures, the hero (Yeats, Crazy Jane, or others) has chosen to be what he is and has deliberately rejected the easy temporal action for the eternal difficult.

Between the early and late poems there is a continuous development. Thomas Parkinson's illuminating study, *W. B. Yeats, Self-Critic* (Berkeley and Los Angeles, 1951), has carefully pointed out the main lines of this development, stressing the crucial importance of Yeats's experience as a playwright in his working out of a truly dramatic lyric. According to Parkinson, the success of the early poems is limited because:

> The potential conflict between time and eternity, personal and impersonal, *anima hominis* and *anima mundi* . . . cannot be explored because Yeats' poetic language is the language of only the *anima mundi*. [p. 49]

In revising his plays Yeats gradually learned to make his drama more effective by representing both sides of his opposition through convincingly impressive adversaries. The merchants who buy up souls in *The Countess Cathleen* are simple representatives of evil. But the king in *On the King's Threshold* and Conchubar in *On Baile's Strand* are opponents worthy of Seanchan and Cuchulain, and the impressiveness of their opposition makes the final passionate moment of the heroes so much the more heroic and passionate and dramatic. As Parkinson says:

> A significant experience is a revelation, but it grows from life as well as transcending life's limits. The circumstantial world may be of subsidiary importance, but its existence is necessary in art as in life; the crisis *joins* the temporal and eternal, so we may assume that to present a significant experience, a work of art must in all honesty and fullness admit the claims of time. [p. 84]

This insight of Yeats had a great effect on his lyric poetry. It led him, as Parkinson shows, to surround his own personality, as it appeared in his poems, with the same degree of circumstantial identification as he gave his dramatic heroes. If the fundamental direction of Yeats's desire is always toward the *anima mundi,* the world of passion in which all men can at their best participate, the increasing vividness of the *anima hominis,* the aggregate of institutional and personal triviality, dramatizes the conflict and gives force and poetic point to the hero's choice of values. And out of this tendency to concretize comes a more precise and earth-bound imagery, a more precise location of heroes, especially of Yeats himself, in place and time, and a greater concern on the part of the poet to reproduce the tone and syntax of ordinary speech.

Yeats's desire to reduce the vagueness in his poetry is reflected in his early letters. He writes to AE in 1904:

> In my *Land of Heart's Desire,* and in some of my lyric verse of that time, there is an exaggeration of sentiment and sentimental beauty which I have come to think unmanly. . . . I have been fighting

> the prevailing decadence for years, and have just got it under foot in my own heart—it is sentiment and sentimental sadness, a womanish introspection. . . . I cannot probably be quite just to any poetry that speaks to me with the sweet insinuating feminine voice of the dwellers in that country of shadows and hollow images. I have dwelt there too long not to dread all that comes out of it. We possess nothing but the will and we must never let the children of vague desires breathe upon it nor the waters of sentiment rust the terrible mirror of its blade. [*Letters,* 434–435]

Elsewhere he tells us:

> Now the very essence of genius, of whatever kind, is precision . . . that life where passion and thought are one. [*Letters,* 360]

> . . . vague forms, pictures, scenes etc. are rather a modern idea of the poetic. . . . I avoid every kind of word that seems to me either 'poetical' or 'modern' and above all I avoid suggesting the ghostly (the vague) idea about a god, for it is a modern conception. All ancient vision was definite and precise. [*Letters,* 343]

And he praises the old Irish poets for their use of exact description of scenery, for their precision about places:

> 'Here at this very spot the fairy woman gave so and so the cup of magic mead. Not there by the hillock but here by the rock' and so on. [*Letters,* 354]

Quotations might, but need not, be multiplied. More important is Yeats's practice, and it follows his theory. His beloved, for example, is in the early work not at all distinguished from others of her pre-Raphaelite kind by her "pearl-pale hand" or her "dim heavy hair" or her "cloud-pale eyelids, dream-dimmed eyes." Rossetti, for example, basing his poems on paintings that he but not his reader could see, was accustomed to describing his women as types, not at all particularized but surrounded by an overwhelming and indeed masterly vagueness:

A deep dim wood; and there she stands
 As in that wood that day: for so
Was the still movement of her hands
 And such the pure line's gracious flow.
And passing fair the type must seem,
Unknown the presence and the dream.
 'Tis she: though of herself, alas!
 Less than her shadow on the grass
Or than her image in the stream. ["The Portrait"]

The early Yeats is just as vague, but in the volume *In the Seven Woods* (1904) he begins here and there to make his beloved more particular. His own experience—not *any* lover's or *any* poet's but his own—is brought in, and the scene from which the poet draws his material is often particularized. In "The Folly of Being Comforted" his beloved's hair is turning gray

And little shadows come about her eyes . . .

The poem that gives its title to the volume concerns an actual place and uses the place name not only of the Seven Woods but of one of them in particular, Pairc-na-lee. The pigeons, bees, and flowers of the poem seem to be inhabitants of this particular place, not merely the traditional paraphernalia of lyrical poems.

But the most striking poem in the volume is "Adam's Curse," in which the poet relates a summer's conversation with his beloved and another woman. Here the scene, the words, the thought, are peculiar to the poet's experience, and the poet himself, for the first time, takes an important part in the action. Being particular, he cannot be all things, as the anonymous "I" can at least pretend to be. The poem presents him as talkative, ironic, and melancholy, and if he is of the three characters the most animated, he is also, because of his more detailed characterization, rather witty than wise. An element of mockery has crept in: our hero is fluent and confident, but his love is not happy; he does most of the talking, but it is the "beautiful mild woman" who makes the most telling remark. In short, Yeats here presents himself, as never before, as an actual human being in an actual situation. We are invited to form a double judgment of him: first, that he is to be mocked for his pretensions; and, second, that he is to be admired for his aspiration.

As he develops further, Yeats continues to make his personae, both himself and others, more specific and actual, and through this particularization he makes their moral situations more dramatic and their moral choices more significant. *The Green Helmet and Other Poems* (1910) contains love poems that further individuate the character of Yeats, although the irony of the presentation is still quite restrained. But the figure of Yeats is beginning to be split up into various roles, and the volume gives us various political poems written from the point of view of the busy dramatist and theatre manager who is attempting to forge a literary tradition for Ireland. In "The Fascination of What's Difficult" the busy man of affairs wishes to be free of all the trivial administrative details involved in running a theatre and to return to the writing of lyric poems. In "At the Abbey Theatre," the playwright is annoyed with the fickleness of his drama's audience. In "These Are the Clouds" one friend comforts another by the thought, equally applicable to himself, that the greatness that endures in spite of severe obstacles is great indeed. The poems, "At Galway Races" and "A Friend's Illness," similarly find consolation from despair at political failure in a surer sense of values than the world knows. The irony, the mockery, in all these poems are restrained, but they are not absent. The difficulties of which the poet complains are petty difficulties, and the poet himself, reaching out toward what is of lasting value, is peevish and impatient at all the tedious little troubles that impede his activity. The imagery and the diction bring home this peevishness:

> There's something ails our colt
> That must, as if it had not holy blood
> Nor on Olympus leaped from cloud to cloud,
> Shiver under the lash, strain, sweat and jolt
> As though it dragged road-metal. My curse on plays
> That have to be set up in fifty ways . . .

And again:

> You say, as I have often given tongue
> In praise of what another's said or sung,
> 'Twere politic to do the like by these;
> But was there ever dog that praised his fleas?

In "All Things Can Tempt Me," the poet again mocks himself:

> When I was young,
> I had not given a penny for a song
> Did not the poet sing it with such airs
> That one believed he had a sword upstairs;
> Yet would be now, could I but have my wish,
> Colder and dumber and deafer than a fish.

The persona's arrogance and casualness are quite amazing; his talk of swords upstairs and his desire to emulate, of all things, a fish, are by nineteenth-century standards quite ludicrous. Yet the sweep of the verse and the willingness of the persona to *seem* absurd give him a solidity, even a dignity, far greater than any that ever accrued to Oisin or Forgael or Aengus.

Responsibilities (1914) makes still more of Yeats the public man, especially as the representative of imagination and culture against the confused bad taste of the Irish crowd—a bad taste that is as lamentable in politics as in art. So "Paudeen," "September 1913," "To a Friend Whose Work Has Come to Nothing," "To a Shade," "A Coat," and, most epigrammatically, "On Those That Hated 'The Playboy of the Western World,'

1907" are all written from the point of view of the intelligent Irishman lamenting or cursing the incorrigible stupidity of the crowd. There are other roles, too, in which Yeats appears: as the aging poet, observing the innocence of childhood; as the aging lover, remembering his love; as the friend of three women, paying them tribute. All these poems further show the poet's less admirable qualities—his impatience, his anger, his dependence on his friends, his advancing age—most of all, perhaps, his ungovernable pride. Yet it is because these qualities are honestly presented that the persona is something more than their sum: through them, in spite of them, he is struggling toward values more permanent than the mere conventional avoidance of such petty vices.

And, indeed, throughout *Responsibilities* wisdom is found in the most improbable places where it is overlooked or despised by commonplace minds. If the Irish crowd is too shallow to see what is of value, it is not in this respect unusual. The beggar in "The Hour Before Dawn" is impervious to the wisdom of the sleepy drunkard. The third old hermit sings, "unnoticed like a bird," as does in effect, in "The Three Beggars," the patient crane, but it is the crane and the third old hermit who best embody wisdom. Even in the two songs to a child Yeats's predictions about the child's future go unheeded:

> But I am old and you are young,
> And I speak a barbarous tongue.

In fact, because of their inability to get a hearing, to find an audience that values their wisdom, the wise are like Father Rosicross,

> All wisdom shut into his onyx eyes.

Wherever the wise man or the man struggling toward wisdom turns, he is ignored or mocked. And it is this opposition between the passionate man and the figure he cuts in the world's eyes which defines Yeats's treatment of his personae.

The mature use of this technique to present both himself and other personae as ironic heroes begins with *The Wild Swans at Coole* (1917) and extends through the rest of his career. Where he himself is the persona the technique is most decisive in those poems in which he presents himself in one or more of his local roles—as poet and craftsman, as Irish statesman, as Irish cultural propagandist, as father, as aging or old man, as friend, as householder, as descendant, as potential ancestor—and so manages the presentation as to make, through the deliberate placing of emphasis on the shortcomings of his hero, the transcending of those weaknesses more heroic. Similarly, where the persona is someone other than Yeats the poems are most effective, as in those which have to do with Crazy Jane or wandering fools, when the human limitations of the persona are carefully brought into ironic juxtaposition with his extrahuman perceptions. Such a technique points up clearly the differences between Yeats's early and late verse. Whereas in his early poems he identifies himself with certain admirable personae in order to associate himself with their perceptions and emotions, in his late work all personae are rather depicted than identified with, and their weaknesses are given along with their profundities in order to emphasize their transcendence of their physical and temperamental limitations. This procedure holds not only for such figures as Crazy Jane, but for Yeats as well, as he appears in his poems. The "I" has become not the person behind the expression of emotion, but a stylized character, the subject of a portrait, whose expressed opinions may, outside the poem, be the opinions of the poet, but who, for the duration of the poem, is the creation of the poet, and whose every word and gesture are dictated by the formal requirements of the poem and not by the felt necessity of making the "I" correspond to the actual poet.

In order to show how this is true, we can analyze two of his late poems, one of which presents a persona that is a formalized version of Yeats himself, and the other a persona that is not Yeats. In "Crazy Jane and the Bishop," the simplest of the group of poems in which she figures, two Janes are juxtaposed—the woman whom the world sees, and the woman who has embodied truth. Her love is condemned by the Bishop, but it was, as Jane knows, not an indecent affair, but an experience of affection ("my dear Jack that's dead"), protectiveness ("Jack . . . / . . . bids me to the oak . . . / And there is shelter under it"), and even dignity ("But a birch-tree stood my Jack"). Jane is, indeed, one of those blessed mortals who have a sense for what endures. But she is a character depicted by Yeats and not merely a mouthpiece for his views. On the contrary, while he supports her against the Bishop, a different persona makes a further comment on her through the two lines of refrain in each stanza, a comment in which Crazy Jane does not share: *"All find safety in the tomb"*; and *"The solid man and the coxcomb."* Where Jane is still busy cursing, another persona—indeed a singer—indicates through these refrains that the particular story here told is only another embodiment of the recurring conflict between public morality and the imaginative individual, and that like all former stories with the same theme it ends, for the time being at least, in the grave. His perspective on the situation is far more broad than Jane's, and his concern in the poem is more with the general problem that Jane's view is not broad enough to see here than with the particular embodiment of the opposition which lies within her purview. The poet chooses Jane because from the point of view of the social hierarchy of modern life Jane is the last person likely to participate in anything eternal. Yeats shows that she does so far more than the supposed guardian of the eternal, and that in her simple integrity, for all her violence and coarseness, she has access to the really valuable. But the whole view of the dramatic lyricist is larger than the view of his character; he allows her to present her own vices and virtues; and he allows a different singer to take a larger view; but he himself, through the full poem, indicates their composite significance.

"Among School Children," on the other hand, is an example of the poem in which Yeats dramatizes himself. Here, visiting a schoolroom, he notes the accomplishments of the children, suddenly thinks of his old love talking about *her* childhood and how her talking about it had brought him and her together. He wonders if she might not have looked exactly like one of these children. He thinks of her "present image" and then realizes that he, too, has grown old. This sends him on to an inquiry into the value of a life in which men grow, in spite of their minds, so shockingly old. What makes it worthwhile? And the answer is: passion. Somehow through that passion out of which are born art, love, religious devotion and maternal affection, men can reach through to what endures through all the changes of times, bodies, and civilizations. "Man," as Yeats wrote at the very end of his life, "can embody truth but he cannot know it." [*Letters*, 922]

So from one thought to another the poem proceeds to sum up Yeats's views of life. It touches on childhood, old age, change, and growth; on love between men and women, on motherhood and religious emotion; on art, philosophy, and public life. And the conclusion is Yeats's own, as far as we can see. But a gentle, or not so gentle, mockery goes on throughout the poem and deepens all the insights. The man who sees all this is a "sixty-year-old smiling public man" who wanders dreamily through a public schoolroom. He is amusingly vain, as when he prides himself on his youthful good looks:

> And I though never of Ledaean kind
> Had pretty plumage once . . .

But he catches himself up and resolves to be genial:

> Better to smile on all that smile, and show
> There is a comfortable kind of old scarecrow.

It is this mild caricature of Yeats, created by deliberately ironic phrasing, who is entrusted with the statement of his most profound beliefs. The result is a further extension of meaning, parallel to the extension that comes about in the poems about Crazy Jane through Yeats's more palpable comments on his persona. The man is divided in two, into the noble passion and the human weakness.

But this divided personality is presented in poetic form by Yeats the poet, who, in his capacity as maker of the poem, surveys both sides of himself. The partial selves are necessary to the poem—they compose his "I" —but the total poem implies the presence behind it of a personality temporarily more unified than this divided self and more powerful than their combination. Yeats, in effect, is more than the sum of the half-selves into which he is divided. The total Yeats is best represented by the total poem and its complex meanings than by the poem's protagonist. For the total poem best realizes the import of Yeats as a person: his stylized vision of life conceived as the recurrent dramatic opposition between what endures and what passes.

If this opposition is constant in Yeats's poetry, its presentation is nowhere more effective than in those poems in which the perceptions of the persona are given ironic emphasis by their terribly *human* source. It is "the foul rag-and-bone shop of the heart" that is, as Yeats says, the source of his images of reality. And Yeats is continually showing us that commerce with eternity is possible, not only in spite of, but indeed through, the actual. Nuns, mothers, poets, and old men must all find images—solid human images—to represent the reality that they cannot reach without some concrete embodiment. And the conflict between the *anima mundi* and the *anima hominis* in which every human being must, in effect, take sides, is not an external conflict like a war, but is constantly being played out within human minds.

Conceived as a battleground between opposing forces of cosmic strength, the human mind is the center of a rich drama that Yeats in his mystical writing described in varying ways. *Per Amica Silentia Lunae*, published in 1918, presents this drama through the relatively simple opposition of the *anima mundi* and the *anima hominis*. The mind of any man has access to the universal mind that is the source of all passion. And as "all things are from antithesis" [*Vision*, 268], there is for each self an "anti-self" that the self struggles to become. The self is that part of man which is involved in everyday activity, in the *anima hominis;* the anti-self is his means of escape from the self into the world of passion. So the sick Synge wrote in a vigorous style about vigorous people,[1] and Keats

> made—being poor, ailing and ignorant,
> Shut out from all the luxury of the world,
> The coarse-bred son of a livery-stable keeper—
> Luxuriant song. [*CP*, 159]

As a constructed self created out of all that is unlike the natural self, and opening the way to the life of passion and meaning, Yeats's anti-self or mask is reminiscent of Oscar Wilde's conception of the mask that, because it was itself a work of art, was a finer guide to truth than the natural self. For Yeats the anti-self, an object of desire rather than a work of art, is characteristically attained through the *making* of works of art, and artists forgo the values of their natural lives for the greater values attainable through the realization of their anti-selves:

> What portion in the world can the artist have
> Who has awakened from the common dream
> But dissipation and despair? [*CP*, 159]

A Vision, although it greatly complicates and greatly elucidates Yeats's view of the world, does not alter his basic conception of the mask. The Mask, now capitalized, is in opposition to the Will (or "natural ego") and varies in its exact significance from age to age. It is, nevertheless, for each man, a part of his Destiny, "Destiny being that which comes to us from within." [*Vision*, 84, 86] And the extent to which he realizes his Destiny through the achievement of his Mask is an index of his success in life.

Nevertheless, the complete realization of the Mask, whatever its advantages, is, from a human point of view, strikingly undramatic. It is through the conflict between Will and Mask, between self and anti-self, that poetry and drama must produce their achievement. And it is, consequently, true to say of Yeats's later poetry that much of the power derives from his belief, and from the arrangement of the elements of his poetry to accord with his belief, that those truths to which man can at all attain must be wrung out of the actual material of human life. The perfection of Byzantium arrives, if it does, only at the end of a long career of hard labor. Art in effect consists of repeated commerce between the trivial stuff of common life and the perfection of the finished product. The images out of which a work of art grows

> Grew in pure mind, but out of what began?
> A mound of refuse or the sweepings of a street,
> Old kettles, old bottles, and a broken can,
> Old iron, old bones, old rags, that raving slut
> Who keeps the till. [*CP*, 336]

Furthermore, the individual personae who are presented as involved in the struggle between two worlds must be carefully dramatized. All the elements of the poetry must be carefully arranged to present the drama of the conflict and of the issuing choice at its most dramatic. In particular, the lyric poem, whatever its history, can no longer be an expression of opinions, ideas, or feelings, but becomes a verbal stage on which the drama of the conflicting opposites plays itself out.

And the lyric "I," like other personae, is not primarily used to stand pronominally for a complex of feelings which is the poet; it is rather one part of a poetic structure designed to present the significant conflict between eternal and temporal values which exists objectively in the common human world.

The personae of the poems are, therefore, continually presented by techniques appropriate to the main aim of the poetry: the delineation of the basic oppositions of the world. That we must always approach more meaningful experience through what seems like trivial experience, is an ironic fact, and Yeats keeps emphasizing the fact even in the form of his work by making those characters who do so approach it peculiar in some way: Crazy Jane, himself, Tom the lunatic, and other characters presented dramatically or referred to in the poems. They must create their triumph out of the dirt of their own lives. To put it another way, our approaches to ecstasy are ludicrous, but there is nothing else to rescue our trivial daily life but such approaches. The best of men waver between absurdity and dignity. And sometimes—in art, in death, in the natural union of man and woman, or even in the living out of certain kinds of passionate lives—the absurdity may dissolve in the dignity.

So in his poems about himself Yeats alternately presents himself as absurd or as passionate. He is "A tattered coat upon a stick," "A foolish, passionate man," "a broken man"; and he is spurred on by "lust and rage." [*CP*, 191, 281, 335, 309] He refers to

> this caricature,
> Decrepit age that has been tied to me
> As to a dog's tail. [*CP*, 192]

His friends, too, are old:

> What images are these,
> That turn dull-eyed away,
> Or shift time's filthy load,
> Straighten aged knees,

Hesitate or stay?
What heads shake or nod? [*CP*, 249]

He makes a point of saying that Lady Gregory is "an aged woman." [*CP*, 238] And in her house there is

Sound of a stick upon the floor, a sound
From somebody that toils from chair to chair.
[*CP*, 239]

Another friend is "withered old and skeleton-gaunt." [*CP*, 229] The emphasis on physical degeneration is everywhere and may be summed up in the lines from "The Curse of Cromwell":

I came on a great house in the middle of the night,
Its open lighted doorway and its windows all alight,
And all my friends were there and made me welcome too;
But I woke in an old ruin that the winds howled through;
And when I pay attention I must out and walk
Among the dogs and horses that understand my talk.
O what of that, O what of that,
What is there left to say?

For Yeats's purposes, the harsher the insistence upon the humanness of himself and his friends and his personae, the greater the triumph in transfiguring that humanness.

On the other hand, the human, with all its limitations, is actually valuable because it makes the conflict, and therefore the triumph, possible. "To me," says Yeats,

all things are made of the conflict of two states of consciousness, beings or persons which die each other's life, live each other's death. [*Letters*, 918]

"All things are from antithesis," he writes elsewhere, and again: "all things fall into a series of antinomies in human experience." [*Vision*, 268, 193] The emphasis on conflict is constant in Yeats, and he embraces it: a fascination with his own infirmities and those of his personae is one aspect of this acceptance; a more explicit statement not only of the welcome he gives to the conflict but of his jubilant acceptance of human limitations is to be found in his poems, notably in "A Dialogue of Self and Soul," "which is," as Yeats has written, "a choice of rebirth rather than deliverance from birth": [*Letters*, 729]

> I am content to live it all again
> And yet again, if it be life to pitch
> Into the frog-spawn of a blind man's ditch,
> A blind man battering blind men;
> Or into that most fecund ditch of all,
> The folly that man does
> Or must suffer, if he woos
> A proud woman not kindred of his soul.
>
> I am content to follow to its source
> Every event in action or in thought;
> Measure the lot; forgive myself the lot!
> When such as I cast out remorse
> So great a sweetness flows into the breast
> We must laugh and we must sing,
> We are blest by everything,
> Everything we look upon is blest.

IV

So sings the earth-bound Self in triumphant opposition to the Soul, which in this poem has urged a renunciation, a transcendence, of the earthly abyss. The Soul finds all its values in the pose, in the mask, or Mask, in the eternal values that transcend the human; but the Self knows that the human must continue to exist vigorously in order for its transcending to have any meaning. Yet the Self, as it is only part of the poem, is only part of the human entity anatomized *in* the poem. The Self and the Soul compose a dramatic conflict that issues in the triumph of the Self. And although the plot of the poem revolves around the human choice of rebirth, its aim is not to present this choice as a type of transcendental experience, but to illuminate the nature of the choice that is to be made. The best way to present human reality is through the experience of persons, but although the experience gives the poem its vitality, the reality it embodies gives the poem its import.

In effect, the self, like the soul—all parts of the psychic life of the person—is seen now from outside. The point of view *in* the poem is that of the persona; the point of view *of* the poem is that of the poet to whom the self and its situation comprise all reality. But as soon as the poet detaches himself from his persona in this way, his focus is on the situation, not on the self. No longer does the self define the universe; no longer is its situation a modification of the self, one aspect of the godlike human creature whose mental events comprise ultimate reality. Now it is the situation that is central, the cosmic and moral situation that includes, as instances, the mental events of specific human beings. The struggle persists, but the point of view with which it is traced changes.

The poet who views the struggle (now the situation) from outside must present it, if not with strict impartiality, at least with a sense of the value of each element. If he looks upon the situation as a drama, he can see the instrumental importance of every component. The struggle between subject and object, seen from the point of view of the subject, must inevitably be distorted, must stress the virtues of subject, the evil of object, or twist in other ways their complex interrelationships, for the aim of art written from this point of view will be to present the experience of the perceiver. But seen from a distance, with detachment, the place of the casual and the enduring, of subject and object, will be presented in proper proportions. The center of the world will be seen to be the human situation, not the human psyche. And the point of view of the poet will be that of the ultimately but not presently involved self, the presently but not ultimately detached observer. This point of view may be permitted to distort the elements of the human situation, but not the situation itself.

In such a poetry, then, the casual will be an indispensable element, for the drama of the human situation must be embodied in a choice between casual and enduring values. The evil, the commonplace, the trivial, must be presented in all their attractiveness if the choosing self's transcendence of them is to be effective. So it is in Yeats's later work: the casual is both attractive and repulsive, but its very attractiveness is its danger, and its repulsive power is a necessary concomitant of its being worth transcending.

The place of the poet-persona must also, in this new poetry, undergo an important change. The poet who now stands aside from the struggle and reports it can enter his poem only ambiguously. He can no longer participate in the old noble persona, nor can he now be even approximately contained within *any* persona. For standing outside the poem he poses his personae, arranges them in ways that will serve his various purposes. If any "I" is noble, he must be ambiguously so: all his shortcomings must be shown not as charming foibles but as significant limitations, regrettable perhaps from the point of view of the "I," but not from that of the poet to whom they are necessary elements of the world's composition and the basis of his own. Such is the pattern of Yeats's personae: he himself, Crazy Jane, and the rest are noble only in their ultimate alignment with eternal values, an alignment to which their infirmities, vices, and follies give point.

But the "I" need have no nobility at all. Since he no longer stands for the poet except nominally, the poet need not be vain of the figure he cuts in the poem.

If the emphasis of poetry is on a recurrent situation, not on the feeling self and its experiences, then the structure of that situation, not the virtues of that self, must be central in the poem. The personae can be therefore completely separate from the poet, and far from noble. Crazy Jane and others are not even diminished, self-mock versions of the poet, nor are they his mouthpieces; they are versions of selves, depicted by the poet, diminished heroes distinct from the poet. And, on the other hand, the poet may present himself or other personae as typical actors of certain roles neither noble nor ignoble, as impersonal observers and perceivers who exist as persons mainly in the sense that they function literally as convenient points of view—indeed as conventional singers similar to those of the Renaissance.

We can note in his criticism as well as in his poetry how strongly Yeats was drawn throughout his career to that formal and stylized presentation of human reality which renders ambiguous the literal assertions of every "I." His main concern at the beginning of the century was to find a form, a style, in which he could adequately present the opposites in his own character and in the world. He writes, in 1909:

> To oppose the new ill-breeding of Ireland . . . I can only set up a secondary or interior personality created out of the tradition of myself, and this personality (alas, only possible to me in my writings) must be always gracious and simple. It must have that slight separation from interests which makes charm possible, while remaining near enough for passion. [*Auto*, 280]

Our examination above of Yeats's early treatment of himself indicates that this is a most inadequate description of the nervous, arrogant "I" of his poems. But a few years later he states his position more carefully in a letter to his father:

> All our art is but the putting our faith and the evidence of our faith into words or forms and our

> faith is in ecstasy. Of recent years instead of 'vision,' meaning by vision the intense realization of a state of ecstatic emotion symbolized in a definite imagined region, I have tried for more self portraiture. I have tried to make my work convincing with a speech so natural and dramatic that the hearer would feel the presence of a man thinking and feeling. [*Letters*, 583]

He has turned, that is, to the depiction of himself as a character in his own poems. So he admires the Japanese artists of whom he says: "In every case the artist one feels has had to *consciously* and deliberately arrange his subject." And in the same letter he remarks on the suggestiveness of rhythm: "If I delight in rhythm I love nature though she is not rhythmical. I express my love in rhythm." [*Letters*, 608]

In his poetic practice Yeats tried to realize the implications of his theoretical ruminations. The increasingly formal structure of his verse is nowadays accepted as a critical commonplace. As early as 1901 he complains that his own verse has been "not plastic enough." "I have to make everything very hard and clear, as it were." [*Letters*, 354, 358] Subsequently, his poems realize with greater and greater accuracy the conflict which he feels is central to the world. Whereas all conflict in the early poems was presented in a smooth, sensuous verse that contained in itself little suggestion of conflict, and through characters whose separation from worldly affairs made their difficulties unconvincing, henceforth Yeats's world would be increasingly reflected both in character and in versification. Bold and sometimes ludicrous images, stately, bare, and jazzed-up rhythms, and characters torn almost comically in two between their human and their cosmic affiliations—these became the elements of the later formal verse of Yeats.

And these elements, fused in a poetic form, were to do more than represent a conflict. If the poem is really to present reality, it must be unified not by the persona (the unity *he* confers is only superficial) but by the presence of the poet felt at every point in it, as reality is the world suffused with the presence of man. Like the dreamy symbolism of an earlier era, poems might serve "as a symbolism to express subjective moods." [*Letters,* 607] Other poets, in earlier ages or even in Yeats's own, had managed to apply the pressure of their own personalities to the elements of their art so that the art had become, as a whole, an expression of their own personalities. Of some of Lady Gregory's work, for example, it could be said "that only one mind could have made it and that everything has a colour and form and sound of that mind." [*Letters,* 452] In Dowson's poems, too, "one feels the pressure of his life behind every line as if he were a character in a play of Shakespeare's." [*Letters,* 548] And of Donne, Yeats tells us:

> the more precise and learned the thought the greater the beauty, the passion; the intricacy and subtleties of his imagination are the length and depths of the furrow made by his passion. [*Letters,* 570]

Criticizing, in 1905, his own play, *The Shadowy Waters,* Yeats says: "There was no internal life pressing for expression through the characters." [*Letters,* 460] A better work, presumably, would be a finer form, in which the words and actions of the characters would serve not to express themselves but as stylized expressions of the internal life of the poet.

It is possible, then, to say of Yeats's late poetry that it is a formalized expression, through the use of techniques of imagery, verse, and character, of the basic conflict between the opposing members of universal antinomies, and of Yeats's self. It is, consequently, both subjective and objective, both personal and impersonal. Art is to him, perhaps, not so much a resolution of the conflict as a preservation of its complexity in a permanent form. "I think with you," Yeats writes to his father, "that the poet seeks truth, not abstract truth, but a kind of vision of reality which satisfies the whole being." [*Letters,* 588] The body of Yeats's poetry is his vision of reality, a formalized, stylized presentation of the human world, and a mark of his response to it.

More than Eliot or Pound or any poet who has written since their time, Yeats's poetic roots are deep in the nineteenth century, and no examination of his poetry can ignore the extent to which he remained loyal to a view of the poetic art which is largely Romantic. In particular the poses and postures that were characteristic of nineteenth-century verse are always important to Yeats. But in his verse they become deliberate, not in order for the poet to emphasize his sophistication or his diabolical nobility or even his incapacity, but in order that they may satisfy the dramatic requirements of Yeats's presentation of the human situation. The poses serve the craftsman, not the man; the poem as mask serves the man. Similarly, the Pateresque interpretation of life as a series of magic moments each of which is to be carefully cultivated for the exquisite sensations it may bring, is never very foreign to Yeats. But in the synthesis of ideas which yields Yeats's later verse, the magic moments, with their emphasis on experience, are replaced by the complex stasis of *A Vision* or of a poem or of a volume of poems or of all his poems taken together, and the emphasis is on form.

Despite his Romantic background, Yeats's later poetry is unquestionably a new product, basically different in its techniques from any nineteenth-century verse in English. It is more conscious verse in the sense that it results from the craftsmanlike arrangement of poetic materials in a form that functions primarily as a whole and only secondarily by its incidental effects. In particular, Yeats's use of personae shows his difference from his predecessors. His picture of himself in his poems is not so much a confession as a depiction; the "I" of his "personal" poems not only speaks his mind but is held up to the view of the audience in each of his many roles, in his earthly, corruptible actuality as well as in his moments of communion with the eternity of passion. He thus combines in his poetry the self as a feeling subject with the self as an object submitted to the observation of the external world. Yet the poem is something more than the depiction of both these selves or part-selves. The poem is a fuller statement by a fuller self of the conditions of life, and the selves that appear in the poetry are instrumental to the framing of such a statement. The gist of the statement, furthermore, is not so much to be traced, article by article, in the words of the poem as it is to be found implicitly in the dramatic disposition of events and personae, of rhythms and diction. The form of the poetry acts out its content.

Yeats himself, discoursing on tragic art, writes: ". . . and if we are painters, we shall express personal emotion through ideal form, a symbolism handled by the generations, a mask from whose eyes the disembodied looks. . . ." [*CA*, 204] The poem is such a mask, freed for personal expression from the adventitious decorations of personal characteristics. And the mask reflects, even contains, this deepest disembodied self of the poet. For Yeats the articulation of a vision of reality serves also as the fulfillment of the poet's personality, the realization of his Mask. Posing not himself but deliberately developed versions of himself and other personae, he presents his view of the human situation. The presentation of this view is expressive of Yeats's personality, for it is—not in its explicit statements but in the very texture of its rhythms, rhymes, imagery, structure, *and* explicit statements—dense with the weight of his intellectual and moral power, of his *person*. The poem, taken as a whole, is the mask through which he speaks, as poet, to his reader; the poem, not the "I," is his voice, his persona.

4

Pound: The God Inside

If the poetry of T. S. Eliot presents scores of people, Ezra Pound's presents hundreds. Sketches, portraits, caricatures, vignettes occupy almost all his work; imagist as he is, concerned to find the right words and rhythms for visual and auditory experiences, his work nevertheless seems, on one level, to be a long gallery of character studies. The people in the gallery are modern and ancient; of China, Greece, Provence, and England; poets, soldiers, business men, goddesses, philosophers. Indeed, the astonishing variety of the people, the experiences, and the tones in *The Cantos* has led many readers to dismiss that poem as a random collection of memorabilia and to regard its apparent artlessness as real ineptitude.

But of all modern poetry Pound's is the hardest to judge accurately. Whereas the work of Eliot, Yeats, and many other modern poets continually reflects the English tradition and seems, in spite of any debts it owes to foreign verse, a development consistent with the English poetic past, Pound's position is quite different. Though he owes much to Browning, the main achievement of his poetry may be the adaptation to English of poetic methods seldom used in English verse. His use of masks and of the dramatic monologue, while essential in his poetry, cannot be understood without a sense of the dynamic structure typical in his poems. As it is a structure heavy with possibilities for future English poetry, its implications are both immense and obscure, but we require some account of it before we can quite grasp the virtues of Pound's writing.

Pound's poetry rests on his rejection of formal rhetorical patterns as the basis of poetic structure. In almost all English poetry an argument leads to a climax; English poets arrange with infinite variety a sequence of climactic sections that eventuate in a principal climax. Although the sections are arranged differently in different genres and in different eras, the typical aim is to arrange a sequence promising completion if the audience will just see it through to its conclusion. In effect, there must be a structure of logical development —a beginning, a middle, and an end—just as in drama, which in its conditions reflects the basic rhetorical situation. The audience must be held. The poet must therefore arouse something in them, set up some kind of temporal suspension that only continued attention can resolve. Virtually all of English fiction, drama, and poetry fulfills this rhetorical pattern.

In fact, so accustomed have we become to the rhetorical structure that we tend to forget that literature can have any other. This is understandable in the light of the practice of most English poets, who have traditionally chosen and composed their poetic units—their stanzas, their sections—in such a way as to emphasize their discursive continuity, to build up toward a climax, to bring home each point with a bang. The climaxes in English poems announce themselves in the verse; it slows down or speeds up, it becomes sonorous or contrastingly simple, it reflects in conventional sound-patterns the resolution of the story or the idea.

Pound's poetry has a different basic structure, intentionally imitative of the structure of certain Chinese and European verse. It might be suggested that the structure is basically textural rather than temporal. In

"The Encounter," for example, the point lies in the way in which the quality of the experience is presented, not in the logical resolution of an idea or story:

> All the while they were talking the new morality
> Her eyes explored me.
> And when I arose to go
> Her fingers were like the tissue
> Of a Japanese paper napkin.

Here the effect is of the fragility and delicacy of the thing said. If the last line comprises a resolution, it is not a resolution of discursive or narrative suspense, but of an incomplete abstract (and humorous) design, like an unresolved musical chord. Or, to take another example of Pound's juxtapositional technique, here is "L'Art, 1910":

> Green arsenic smeared on an egg-white cloth,
> Crushed strawberries! Come, let us feast our eyes.

In both poems the climax defeats our expectations and reveals to us a fuller meaning in what has gone before. But there is no fanfare, no sonority, no straightforward moving to a conventional poetic climax. The poems resist our attempts to make out of the actual an occasion for conventional emotionality. They stand out against the poem conceived as a convenient receptacle for stale emotions. And they do this mainly by becoming arrangements of textures rather than series of logically continuous meanings. The textural units of his longer poems build up no suspense; rather, they create larger textural units whose aim is to convey the quality of human response to the world.

Joseph Frank, in his well-known essay, "Spatial Form in Modern Literature,"[1] has described the tendency of twentieth-century writers to make the reader wait until he has finished the poem and then go back to survey all of it as a whole in a single moment, as if it were spread out in space. To some extent, this is true of all poetry written by poets who are conscious of the total effect of their work, as every poet must partially be.

The temporal continuity from event to event becomes immobilized in a perspective that is, in effect, that of eternity. And, at least in our own age, all poems make more sense to us when we see them finally in this way.

But at the same time, almost all poems are written, and deserve to be read, in a different fashion as well. The progress from point to point is significant. To put it another way, the reader must share not only the perspective of the total poem, but also the incidental perspectives along the way. Personae are the instruments for setting up these perspectives, and all poets must take advantage of the perspectives they provide. Even Eliot, Yeats, and Pound, though their chief perspective is the total one, rely largely on personae to establish convenient perspectives through which the poet can guide the reader to some fuller perspective. And even Eliot and Yeats are in danger of having the attitudes of their personae mistaken for their own at the same time that their poems are admired as poems. But take *The Cantos* in this way, take his personae for Pound and their attitudes for his, and the poem is likely to seem both meaningless and distasteful. The only way of reading *The Cantos* and such poems of Pound as the two cited above, is to grasp them as textural units, to see them as subtle poetic realizations of the *feel* of human experience.

If we look for action, for a story, for any suspense but that resulting from an incomplete design, we read the poem by an aesthetic that cannot contain it. Stories may exist *in* it, and certainly *The Cantos* presents an abundance of history. But not *as* history, not as continuous or even continual development. *The Cantos* requires to be read, through all its hundreds of pages, as an image, as "an intellectual and emotional complex" comprehended "in an instant of time." [*LE*, 4] In order to present this complex, Pound employs personae, chiefly himself, as convenient points of view, just as the masks of his earlier poems conveniently provide illuminating perspectives. But the perspectives are useful only as instruments; the fundamental perspective is that which reader and poet share on the entire poem, that from which reader and poet undergo a single and unified experience of a many-textured world.

II

Like other modern poets, Pound characteristically allows his personae to speak in conversational language. If there is anything he despises in the English tradition, it is pompous sonority, and probably no poet in English has so successfully steered clear of it. His characters often bluster and swagger, but they speak in the most man-to-man fashion and usually with a strong mixture of colloquial terms. In fact, good conversation is one of Pound's most frequently discussed values, and his personae delight to engage in it. They talk, as one of them says in Canto XI,

> Both of ancient times and our own; books, arms,
> And of men of unusual genius,
> Both of ancient times and our own, in short the
> usual subjects
> Of conversation between intelligent men.

If poetry is speech to any poet, it is so to Pound. True, in his early poems some of his personae occasionally grow rather Romantically pompous, like the Poet in "And Thus in Nineveh":

> 'It is not, Raana, that my song rings highest
> Or more sweet in tone than any, but that I
> Am here a Poet, that doth drink of life
> As lesser men drink wine.'

No faith could be more Wordsworthian. But this kind of contempt for the audience is rare. A more colloquial contempt for audience or interlocutor occurs oftener, but it is hardly the kind of contempt that makes the reader feel oppressed by the virtuous superiority of the persona:[2]

O generation of the thoroughly smug
and thoroughly uncomfortable . . . [94]

Ha! sir, I have seen you sniffling and snoozling
about among my flowers . . .
[120]

You whoreson dog, Papiols, come! Let's to music!
[42]

And familiar to every reader of Pound are the many passages of satiric invective:

All for one half-bald, knock-knee'd king of the
Aragonese,
Alfonso, Quattro, poke-nose. [36]

Go, my songs, to the lonely and the unsatisfied,
Go also to the nerve-racked, go to the enslaved-
by-convention. . . .

Go to the bourgeoise who is dying of her ennuis,
Go to the women in suburbs.
Go to the hideously wedded,
Go to them whose failure is concealed,
Go to the unluckily mated,
Go to the bought wife,
Go to the woman entailed. [97]

But passages like these have little unpleasant effect. Humor is never very far away even at Pound's most serious moments; and two later lines from the last poem quoted above indicate the usual tone of his verse:

Go in a friendly manner,
Go with an open speech.

Pound's personae generally, for all their contempt and anger and indignation directed against evil, speak in a friendly manner and openly to, or in the presence of, the reader. There is much to hate, but hate is part of what one expresses in talk, and the speech of Pound's personae is usually engaging, quaint, colorful, or simply moving, and good-natured even in gloom.

There is no stand-offishness about Pound's personae. They meet the reader as equals with but rare exceptions. They speak in conversational tones—animated or hushed. Whether the "I" stands for Pound or any of his hundreds of other speakers, the tones deliberately abhor those rhetorical patterns that remove the speaker from intimacy with the listener. Thus, not only is the diction (even where it is archaic) essentially conversational, but so (recurrently if not continuously) are the sound-patterns of the speeches. Exclamations, self-interruptions, sentence fragments and other grammatical peccadilloes common in speech but usually avoided in writing, fill the pages of this poetry of talk. His own poetry meets Pound's requirement that nothing should appear in a poem which we could not imagine someone saying under the pressure of some emotion.

III

Writing about his own work in 1916, Pound divides his poems into three groups:

> In the 'search for oneself,' in the search for 'sincere self-expression,' one gropes, one finds some seeming verity. One says 'I am' this, that, or the other, and with the words scarcely uttered one ceases to be that thing.
>
> I began this search for the real in a book called *Personae,* casting off, as it were, complete masks of the self in each poem. I continued in long series of translations, which were but more elaborate masks.
>
> Secondly, I made poems like 'The Return,' which is an objective reality and has a complicated sort of significance, like Mr. Epstein's 'Sun God,' or Mr. Brzeska's 'Boy with a Coney.' Thirdly, I have written 'Heather,' which represents a state of consciousness, or 'implies,' or 'implicates' it. . . .

These two latter sorts of poems are impersonal . . . [*GB*, 98]

By the time he wrote these words, Pound's aesthetic was fairly well worked out. His three most important poems, to be sure, postdate this statement, but not by long, for *Homage to Sextus Propertius* was published in 1919, *Hugh Selwyn Mauberley* in the following year, and the first version of *Three Cantos* appeared in *Poetry* during 1917. In any case, the three "sorts of poems" outlined above had already been established, and the achievement of his greater poetry would lie in its combination and organization of these techniques. The poem which is a mask, the poem "which is an objective reality," and the poem "which represents a state of consciousness"—these are basic instruments of the poetry of Pound. They exist separately in his early short poems; the later work combines them into an orchestra.

The mask poems seem the simplest and the most traditional in their point of view. But to understand Pound's masks and how they change in the course of his career is to understand much about his poetry. The strange and rather undramatic structure of his poems is consistent with his enduring indifference to the theatre. Yet hardly any nondramatic poet has ever been so concerned with people or has put so many speeches into the mouths of such widely varied characters. Paradoxically, too, it was Pound who brought into prominence the very word *persona,* who used it as the title of several of his volumes, and who has discussed masks and personae as among his basic poetic techniques. To be sure, the word had long been familiar to all readers of dramatic literature, but rather in its derivative meaning of "person" than in the sense of "mask." Pound returned to the word its old connotations. Along with later critics he has used mask and persona to describe the role a poet takes when he pretends to have another character speak in verse. On such occasions the poet still speaks, but he speaks through a mask. Although poets have always used this technique, and although it is one purpose of this study to assert that every poem must use it to some degree, Pound's theory and practice relate specifically to the variation employed in the dramatic monologue.

Browning is the English poet from whom Pound learned most, and Browning's dramatic monologues are a primary source of Pound's poetry. Like Browning's, Pound's personae just talk and talk, and in the process they reveal something that the reader sees more fully than the persona. But there are differences between the two poets. Browning's personae are often not altogether admirable fellows, but Pound's almost always are, perhaps exactly because they *can* converse, and only the good possess that talent. The result is that the reader sympathizes more fully with Pound's personae than with Browning's. Then, too, although sometimes they address their talk to specific persons, Pound's personae usually speak, as Browning's do not, to a rather vague and general public, sometimes small, sometimes of uncertain size; the emphasis is thus less on the persona's specific situation than on his general relation to the world around him.

But the differences go deeper. According to Pound, he composed these masks "in the search for 'sincere self-expression.'" The poet is trying to find a speech that will express him. One way of doing this is to find or create a character with whom one feels a special affinity, and, in representing his temperament and attitudes, to express one's own. Thus, in assuming the masks of Cino, Arnaut de Marvoil, Bertran de Born, and other old Provençal and Italian poets, Pound in his early volume *Personae* (1909) recreates their dramatic situations and finds an English that is an equivalent of the language they once spoke. The association of poet with persona is reminiscent of early Romantic verse, but the main difference between Pound's personae and those of Byron, Shelley, and Keats is that Pound does not create a fictional character or rejuvenate a legendary one in his own image; rather, like Browning, he tries to reproduce the spirit of an actual historical figure. Unlike Browning, he chooses figures with whose attitudes he can associate his own. But Pound's eventual conviction of the inadequacy of the mask as a means of self-expression seems to indicate his awareness that the more accurate the presentation of the historical persona, the less he can stand for the poet.

But there is more to it still. The sympathetic modern recreation of an old historical figure implies, or can imply, the permanent validity of that figure's attitudes. But the poet cannot recommend old attitudes without recreating them in modern form. To some extent he can find modern instances of admirable attitudes, but they are bound to lack scope unless the poet can place them against a background that vividly presents "examples of civilization," momentous personalities occurring through the ages. This, of course, is what Pound eventually does in *The Cantos*, and his early work mostly revolves around the problem of recreating old figures with their attitudes intact. How does the poet convert their archaic essence into contemporary meaning?

For although reader and poet may sympathize with an historical persona, they know that modern Europe is not medieval Provence, that almost a thousand years have passed since Guillaume of Poitiers began to write modern lyrics, and that Dante, Shakespeare, and Browning have among others written since. Reader and poet inevitably share a perspective that the persona cannot share. This means that the sympathetic persona is either a pretty picture or else meaningful because his attitudes are still valid. But his attitudes cannot be valid today unless contemporary conditions have not essentially changed. In fact, the poet can make his old personae meaningful only by showing the contemporaneity of the past, by showing that human reality is much the same in any age.

The mask, therefore, can be no simple technique. Both reader and poet must be aware that the historical virtues of old personae are currently meaningful, must recognize that Cino and Bertran de Born were struggling against a vice and corruption that are still part of the human world. The mask that the poet assumes must carry with it a meaning unavailable to the persona. The twentieth-century poet speaks through the twelfth- or fourteenth-century poet, augmenting the consciousness of the latter with his own superior awareness. The speaker is aware only of his own world, but the words he speaks have reference to much more.

This "more" of the words leads Pound into his lifelong concern with translation. He himself, as he says, after his initial experiments with masks, proceeded to "long series of translations, which were but more elaborate masks," and which eventually taught him how to get that "more," that increase of import, into the words of the speaker, and thus to change the reader's response from full identification to sympathetic understanding and appreciation of the persona's significance. For Pound translations are of two kinds. There are those that try to "interpret" the work to the reader, and in these the translator

> is in all probability impotent to do *all* of the work for the linguistically lazy reader. He can show where the treasure lies, he can guide the reader in choice of what tongue is to be studied, and he can very materially assist the hurried student who has a smattering of a language and the energy to read the original text alongside the metrical gloze. [*LE*, 200]

In the other kind of translation the translator "is definitely making a new poem," and this, if it is good, "falls simply in the domain of original writing."

Both kinds of translations may serve as masks. The

first kind, exemplified by Pound's translations of Arnaut Daniel and Guido Cavalcanti, enables the poet and student to enter into the spirit of the original poem and, through recognition of the impossibility of adequate translation, to appreciate what there is in the original. The second kind of translation is, for our purposes, more important. Through it the translator associates himself with the original poet, and yet attempts to create, as well as he can, a new poem based on the old, but richer because of its extra dimension, because the association in a similar emotion of two poets who write in different languages and ages adds a complexity not in the original. As Pound says later of his *Homage to Sextus Propertius:*

> . . . it presents certain emotions as vital to me in 1917, faced with the infinite and ineffable imbecility of the British Empire, as they were to Propertius some centuries earlier, when faced with the infinite and ineffable imbecility of the Roman Empire. These emotions are defined largely, but not entirely, in Propertius' own terms. . . . I certainly omitted no means of definition that I saw open to me, including shortenings, cross cuts, implications derivable from other writings of Propertius. . . . [*Letters,* 231]

Good translations, according to Pound, are usually of this order. Pope, for example, does not give us the original, but "he has at least the merit of translating Homer into *something.*" [*LE,* 250] But the best English translations are earlier than Pope. Gavin Douglas' *Eneados* and Golding's translation of Ovid's *Metamorphoses* are the brightest spots in English translation, mostly because the translators assumed, to some extent, the mask of their masters: "The quality of translations declined in measure as the translators ceased to be absorbed in the subject matter of their original." [*LE,* 247] Sometimes, as in Douglas' work, the translation is better than the original. In any case, the assumption of the task of translation is not an exercise in the substitution of words in one language for words in another, but an imaginative, if tentative, identification of the translator with the original writer; in this identification the translator shares the interests, the outlook, the feelings, of his author. But, further, he becomes, in a sense, the twentieth-century self of his author. In assuming the mask of the old poet, he becomes both writers at once, and through the contemporary idiom of the words an intelligence speaks which is greater than the single-dimensioned intelligence of either. The persona consists of two persons and is alternately the original poet and the old poet augmented by the new poet's sense of the old. At the same time, since persona and superior consciousness tend to coincide, the poem is reminiscent of similar Romantic poems, in which the reader is invited to associate his own feelings and responses with those of the persona. But it more closely resembles the juxtaposed profile and full face of Picasso's people. We project ourselves doubly into the persona—into the apparent old poet, and into his modern counterpart. Gradually in Pound's work the emphasis shifts from the re-creation of character to the significance of the re-creation, and his own projective energy undergoes a similar shift from the point of view of the persona to the point of view implied by the augmentation of the persona. Not the old speaker but his modern significance, is what the reader must ultimately see.

In Pound's later work the masks grow even more complex, as they comprise only parts of larger poetic units devoted to the presentation of the *feel* of reality, of intellectual as well as of sensory and emotional reality. The persona becomes, in the first instance, the ancient speaker; in the second, the speaker augmented by the new poet's sense of him; and, in the third, both these faces, taking their place in the larger textural unit of which they are a part, and ultimately in the whole poem. The reader must alter the apparent persona in the light of all these further considerations, and identify himself with each in turn but most of all with the last, with the whole poem as it turns its complex illumination at once on the persona and on the persona's significance.

IV

After his early poems and translations, according to Pound, he moved on to a further phase:

> Secondly, I made poems like 'The Return,' which is an objective reality and has a complicated sort of significance, like Mr. Epstein's 'Sun God,' or Mr. Brzeska's 'Boy with a Coney.' [*GB*, 98]

"The Return" reads as follows:

> See, they return; ah, see the tentative
> Movements, and the slow feet,
> The trouble in the pace and the uncertain
> Wavering!
>
> See, they return, one, and by one,
> With fear, as half-awakened;
> As if the snow should hesitate
> And murmur in the wind,
>   and half turn back;
> These were the 'Wing'd-with-Awe,'
>   Inviolable.
>
> Gods of the wingèd shoe!
> With them the silver hounds,
>   sniffing the trace of air!
>
> Haie! Haie!
>   These were the swift to harry;
> These the keen-scented;
> These were the souls of blood.
>
> Slow on the leash,
>   pallid the leash-men!

In order to discover in what way such a poem is "an objective reality," we may see what Gaudier-Brzeska says about his "Boy with a Coney," to which Pound compares his poem:

> [This piece] has been referred to . . . as an echo of the bronze animals of the Chow dynasty. It is better than they. They had, it is true, a maturity brought by continuous rotundities—my statuette has more monumental concentration—a result of the use of flat and round surfaces. To be appreciated is the relation between the mass of the rabbit and the right arm with that of the rest. [*GB*, 27]

Pound's poem, like Gaudier's work, then, is to be thought of in terms of rotundities, of flat and round surfaces, of relations between masses. Gaudier's piece is an objective reality because it stands in space and is a modification of space. Pound's poem is to be thought of in some such way, as an arrangement of words, a form, the presence of which in the world modifies the world. As the earlier masks attained greater complexity, and as the "I" in the persona became increasingly ambiguous and hence increasingly objective, Pound began to write these new poems, like "The Return," poems that, as objective realities, were forms complete in themselves, the "sculpture of rhyme." "Great works of art," writes Pound, ". . . cause form to come into being." [*GB*, 106]

The arrangement of these forms, however, is not cut off from the feeling of the artist. As Gaudier-Brzeska says:

> I SHALL DERIVE MY EMOTIONS SOLELY FROM THE ARRANGEMENT OF SURFACES, I shall present my emotions by the ARRANGEMENT OF MY SURFACES, THE PLANES AND LINES BY WHICH THEY ARE DEFINED. [*GB*, 20]

And elsewhere Gaudier says of the modern sculptor that "what he feels he does so intensely and his work is nothing more nor less than the abstraction of this intense feeling." [*GB*, 35] Pound himself compares art works to the equations of mathematics, but with a significant difference:

> By the 'image' I mean such an equation; not an equation of mathematics, not something about *a*, *b*, and *c*, having something to do with form, but about *sea, cliffs, night,* having something to do with mood. [*GB*, 106]

And, finally, "Art is more interesting [than mathematics] in proportion as life and the human consciousness are more complex and more interesting than forms and numbers." [*GB*, 106]

From these statements by Gaudier and Pound it seems clear that a poem like "The Return" is an objective reality in the sense that it stands as an independent form that is a presentation of certain emotions of the poet. It is an arrangement of surfaces, of moods, into a whole that somehow gives a whole feeling. "The Return" is a poem about deterioration, and it shows a careful arrangement of surfaces. The hesitating rhythms, the short phrases, and the choice of the words which set the moods (tentative, slow, uncertain, wavering, fear, hesitate, half turn back—these on the one hand, and, on the other, Wing'd-with-Awe, inviolable, wingèd shoe, silver hounds, Haie, swift to harry, keen-scented) are all delicately disposed—Pound has one ear to the rhythms of modern French poetry—to effect the poem's basic contrast between what was and what is. If the poem is successful, then the effecting of the contrast is an objective reality and an abstraction of the poet's feeling about degeneration. The poem objectifies a mood of the poet and invites the reader to share that mood.

"Thirdly, I have written 'Heather,' which represents a state of consciousness, or 'implies,' or 'implicates' it." [*GB*, 98] The poem, "Heather," follows:

> The black panther treads at my side,
> And above my fingers
> There float the petal-like flames.

> The milk-white girls
> Unbend from the holly-trees,
> And their snow-white leopard
> Watches to follow our trace.

"Heather" is no less a formal structure than "The Return," but to Pound in 1916 the emphasis was slightly different. And the difference is clearer in the light of his conception of the image, for he says of "Heather" and "The Return": "These two latter sorts of poems are impersonal. . . . They are Imagisme." [*GB*, 98]

"An 'Image'," Pound writes, "is that which presents an intellectual and emotional complex in an instant of time." [*LE*, 4] In this sense the word applies both to the individual images that the poet uses in his poem, and to the poem itself which exists as a whole complex comprehended in an instant of time. Both kinds of images do the same job, but it is important to distinguish between them. Pound's well-known Metro image is as complete in its way as *The Cantos* is in its. The faces comprise one image, although even here the faces are reducible to this face and this face and that face and so on; the image of the petals is also analyzable into more distinct images; and the juxtaposition of these two composite images, in a form whose word order, rhythm, and sound, are appropriate, yields the image that is the poem. As Pound says of Dante: "to him two blending thoughts give a music perceptible as two blending notes of a lute." [*SR*, 177] Here the blending of two images gives a music that is a third image, and the third image is the poem. *The Cantos* only applies this principle of combination on a larger scale.

Images that are satisfactory are what Pound calls "hard" or "true." They correspond in some way to an internal or external reality, or to a combination of them. Gautier, for example,

> is intent on being 'hard'; is intent on conveying a certain verity of feeling, and he ends by being truly poetic. . . . an intentness on the quality of

> the emotion to be conveyed makes for poetry. [*Inst*, 6]

Consequently, the first aim of poetry must be: "Direct treatment of the 'thing' whether subjective or objective." [*LE*, 3] It is a favorite theme of Pound's:

> A poem is supposed to present the truth of passion. [*Letters*, 18]

> Bad art is inaccurate art. It is art that makes false reports. [*LE*, 43]

> By good art I mean art that bears true witness, I mean the art that is most precise. You can be wholly precise in representing a vagueness. [*LE*, 44]

> I take it as the supreme reward for an artist; the supreme return that his artistic conscience can make him after years spent in its service, that the momentum of his art, the sheer bulk of his processes . . . should heave him out of himself, out of his personal limitations . . . and leave him simply the great true recorder. [*Inst*, 112–113]

But art is more than a transcript of reality internal or external. What makes it more valuable than an accurate photograph, for example, is the feeling of the artist, not as it is confessed by his persona, but as it is diffused through his work. In his essay on "Cavalcanti," Pound contrasts Greek and Tuscan sculpture. Greek sculpture is plastic, the result of close study of the human form, but the study is always somewhat abstract, limited (Pound thinks) by a failure to sense the importance of the body to the mind. On the other hand:

> The Tuscan demands harmony in something more than the plastic. He declines to limit his aesthetic to the impact of light on the eye. It would be misleading to reduce his aesthetic to terms of

music, or to distort the analysis of it by analogies to the art of sonority. Man shares plastic with the statue, sound does not require a human being to produce it. The bird, the phonograph, sing. Sound can be exteriorized as completely as plastic. There is the residue of perception, perception of something which requires a human being to produce it. Which even may require a certain individual to produce it. This really complicates the aesthetic. You deal with an interactive force: the *virtu* in short. [*LE*, 151–152]

In such a view men's bodies are allowed, encouraged, to contribute to the intellect, are, in fact, inseparable from men's thoughts. And the fused response of the whole man to his subject matter eventuates in a diffusion of the artist's personality through his work:

Out of these fine perceptions, or subsequent to them, people say that the Quattrocento, or the sculpture of the Quattrocento, discovered 'personality.' All of which is perhaps rather vague. We might say: The best Egyptian sculpture is magnificent sculpture; but its force comes from a non-plastic idea, i.e. the god is inside the statue.

. . . The god is inside the stone, *vacuos exercet aera morsus.* The force is arrested, but there is never any question about its latency, about the force being the essential, and the rest 'accidental' in the philosophic technical sense. The shape occurs.

There is hardly any debate about the Greek classical sculpture, to them it is the plastic that matters. In the case of the Etruscan Apollo at Villa Giulia (Rome) the 'god is inside,' but the psychology is merely that of an Hallowe'en pumpkin. . . .

This sculpture with something inside, revives in the Quattrocento portrait bust. But the antecedents are in verbal manifestation. [*LE*, 152–153]

In the poems of Cavalcanti there is something inside. In those of Petrarch that something is lost, and we have instead a poetry of ornament where the particular ornaments do just as well in one poem as in another. And so:

> We appear to have lost the radiant world where one thought cuts through another with clean edge, a world of moving energies '*mezzo oscuro rade,*' '*risplende in sè perpetuale effecto,*' magnetisms that take form, that are seen, or that border the visible, the matter of Dante's *paradiso,* the glass under water, the form that seems a form seen in a mirror, these realities perceptible to the sense, interacting, '*a lui si tiri*'. . . . [*LE,* 154]

All this that was lost is what Pound attempted to get back again.

This kind of poem—which requires "a certain individual to produce it," in which the world and the self interact to create a form out of the interdependent energies of both, in which meaning and image, substance and *virtu,* move inseparably—is what Pound is working toward. He appears to have in mind a poem that reports reality accurately, but a reality that is the product of the interaction of human and nonhuman energies; and for the bodying forth of such a reality, in the last analysis even the words, the medium, the plastic, does not matter: what matters is what is inside, the substance that through the honest work of the poet achieves verbal manifestation. To make too great a distinction between one's internal world or the life of one's time as possible subjects is to approach irrelevance, for as long as the poet concentrates on the reality of either, he is still objective, still giving verbal manifestation to "the radiant world where one thought cuts through another with clean edge, a world of moving energies." The surrealistic effects of "Heather" are an equation for one aspect of the sensibility of the poet; they put into objective form a state of consciousness, a mood. But the emphasis is not, or should not be, on the fact that the consciousness is Pound's and not someone else's. The poet must not pose or present himself pathetically. As Pound tells us in one of his early letters:

> No art ever yet grew by looking into the eyes of the public. . . . You can obliterate yourself and mirror God, Nature, or Humanity but if you try to mirror yourself in the eyes of the public, woe be unto your art. [*Letters,* 4]

And in his essay on Eliot he uses an epigraph from Remy de Gourmont:

> Il n'y a de livres que ceux où un écrivain s'est raconté lui-même en racontant les moeurs de ses contemporains—leurs rêves, leurs vanités, leurs amours, et leurs folies. [*Inst,* 196]

By concentrating on his job as recorder, as the style-conscious recorder who finds the appropriate form for what he records, the poet will find his own passion, too, involved and expressed.

In his early poetry Pound, using the method of the mask, associates his emotions with those of his personae in an attempt to find himself. But as the modern consciousness gradually supersedes the mask, the mask tends to become an objective reality of which the poet makes use. Mask poems and others come to function as modifications of the objective world, as arrangements of surfaces, and as "impersonal" formal correlatives of the poet's emotion. Furthermore, the sense in which the poem is expressive of the poet's feeling is clarified by Pound's belief that the form of the best art is pervaded with the projected personal force of its creator—the *virtu* of the poet which, projected, becomes also the poem's *virtu,* its substance, its god inside.

Throughout the later poetry of Pound the god remains inside. The plastic form is quickened by the presence of a human consciousness whose creative power arranges the surfaces of this world into new objective realities, and these objective realities are pervaded with the feeling of the poet. Whether or not the poems are written in the first person is not of great importance to this aesthetic. Pieces of sculpture, paintings, and architecture may have the god inside, but they are not executed in the first or in any person. The poet may choose to write in the first person, but his choice will be dictated by the impersonal requirements of his material, just as his arrangement of rhythms, vocabulary, scenes, and other elements of form is dictated by his sense of the totality of whatever has to be said. From this point of view the word "I" in poetry is comparable to the vantage point from which a landscape or portrait is painted, or to the key that gives a musical piece its tonality. It defines a perspective from which the subject matter of the poem, internal or external, can be "objectively" approached, and from which the still more fundamental substance of the poem, reality itself, can be submitted to verbal focus.

V

Speaking of imagism, Pound has said that "certain men move in phantasmagoria; the images of their gods, whole countrysides, stretches of hill land and forest, travel with them." [*Inst*, 234] If we extend the term to include the elements of poetic composition habitual to a particular poet, we may say that the use of the first person in much of Pound's poetry is part of his "phantasmagoria." It is not essential to his view of poetry, but an idiosyncratic method. What is more important is the kind of situation in which the "I," in common with other characters who are referred to in the third person, appears in Pound's poetry. The recurring situation in Pound's work, from beginning to end, places a single individual, whose character may be roughly defined by such words as sensitive, intelligent, strong, honest, active, civilized, passionate, against a background (frequently intruding into the foreground) of a world whose character may be roughly defined by such words as stupid, unfeeling, corrupt, shallow, ignorant, and passionless. This situation is so habitual to Pound that we cannot imagine his poetry without it. If it is possible to speak of a recurrent situation as defining a poet's world, then this situation defines the world of Pound.

To present this situation in poetic form, Pound's poems after 1915 or so employ his earlier techniques in different combinations and explore the possibilities inherent in them from the start. In *Homage to Sextus Propertius* Pound loosely translates his Latin originals and in so doing makes an original poem of his own in which the central irony is the aptness with which the Roman's emotions are applied to the world of 1919. To point this out, with subtle tact and force, making use of his developed poetic equipment, especially of the translation mask, is to make a poem, an objective reality that is the equation for certain of Pound's emotions. Pound's consciousness here so far exceeds that of his persona that the latter has in effect become part of the scenery of the poem, the background against which the objective poem makes its most important contribution to the reader's consciousness. In the series of poems, "Moeurs Contemporaines," Pound, with one eye on the statement of theory of Remy de Gourmont quoted above and with the other on the practice of Gautier and other "hard" French poets, analyzes the corrupt or passionless world into individual persons. These poems are written from the point of view of a persona who presents the material with an impersonal left hand while loading the case with his right, as in Eliot's "Preludes." And the result is again intended to be an objective correlative of Pound's feeling about the world, not merely a series of valid statements.

Hugh Selwyn Mauberley represents Pound's most eccentric use of masks. To determine exactly who speaks the various parts of this enigmatic poem is a puzzle that has long occupied the lucubrations of Pound critics. It now appears that Pound himself considers the first poem, "E. P. Ode pour l'Election de Son Sepulchre," to be spoken by Mauberley himself: ". . . Mauberley buried E. P. in the first poem; gets rid of all his troublesome energies." So he writes to Thomas E. Connolly, who therefore suggests[3] that Mauberley speaks the first twelve poems and the "Envoi," whereas the last five poems form an account of Mauberley's career and a final judgment thereon, rendered by the hostile or indifferent world of letters. Thus, while Mauberley disdainfully damns the literary world, the literary world damns him with equal disdain. The whole presentation forms what John J. Espey has called "an elaborate metrical exercise in the form of a condensed James novel,"[4] in which the inherent weaknesses of Mauberley are made clear—lack of energy, "Irresponse to human aggression," sexual impotency, and imperceptiveness—as well as the weakness of his society. As a compressed novel, the poem certainly leaves much to be desired, but its aim is largely realized even if few readers can penetrate its obscurities; the aim is to present in all their inadequacy certain wrongheaded views of art as they connect with certain wrongheaded views of life.

The matter, buried in almost unfathomable obliquities, is surely unequal to the magnificence of the versification, but *Mauberley* is notable for its treatment of personae. If the above interpretation is correct, Pound's presence in the poem is almost entirely implicit. Never overtly appearing—a rare event for Pound when the setting is a modern one—the poet sympathizes both with Mauberley's and with the literary world's condemnation of each other. The reader is to sense and to share the ironic delight with which the poet, buried at the beginning, hears his two antagonists learnedly, judiciously, and pitilessly destroy each other. This implicit poet is the consciousness to which the reader can join his own—a consciousness hardly present, but only implicit as the point from which the poem is intelligible. The poem is an objective reality, the masks are instrumental, and the god is almost literally inside.

It should be noted in support of this interpretation that the personae of *Mauberley* have an occasional preciousness rarely to be found in Pound's work. Their obscure allusions, their pompous tones, may make somewhat better sense if we understand that, while Pound sympathizes with the burden of what each speaker says, yet at the same time he ridicules both of them for their stuffiness. Even the rhyme and rhythm at their most effective usually have so much humor to them that they confirm the idea that the poem is a learned satire. Against this interpretation stands the fact that in some of the poems—IV, V, and "Mr. Nixon," especially—we can scarcely believe that Mauberley is speaking and not Pound. One way of explaining this difficulty is to suggest that Pound so clearly identifies with some of Mauberley's attitudes that the two become quite confused, but such an explanation is hardly a defense of the poem. I suspect that the Jamesian novel was not Pound's forte, and he wisely abandoned it after *Mauberley*. The poem is almost alone among Pound's efforts in possessing, or pretending to possess, a structure not dominantly textural. It is the only one in which Pound has to use at length modern personae other than himself, and their attitudes are, by any reading I have seen, neither clear nor consistent. The poem is also a rarity in that its personae are mainly unpleasant. Pound, it appears, ventured too far away from the techniques he knew how to handle, and all the splendor of the versification can do little to counter the judgment, by this reader at least, that the poet was wise to return to *The Cantos* and a poetry of which he was already becoming a master.

For it is in *The Cantos* that Pound develops most fully his varieties of personae, using quotations and translations freely to take their places in a plotless but richly textured poem. Throughout the poem, too, there runs the voice of the persona who represents Pound himself, recording the truth of passion and the twentieth-century world. All these instruments are pressed into the service of the poem, and in order to show more concretely how Pound deals with human personality in *The Cantos,* we may examine one of his principal characters, Sigismondo Malatesta, whose personality and fortunes are important to Pound largely because of Sigismondo's one great artistic achievement: the construction, unfinished but distinguished, of the Tempio Malatestiano at Rimini.

John Drummond, in his essay, "The Italian Background to *The Cantos,*" contributed to *An Examination of Ezra Pound,*[5] gives a useful one-paragraph summary of Sigismondo's career:

> The Tempio represents the highest achievement of Humanism; Sigismondo Pandolfo Malatesta, its creator, was the most representative personality of his time, and he remains the dominating personality of *The Cantos.* He lived from 1417 to 1468. A professional *condottieri,* he already, at the age of eighteen, commanded the Papal armies in Romagna and the Marches, and he took part in all the wars in Italy for the next thirty years, first in the service of one *signoria,* then of another, making war in between times on his own account against his life-long rival, Federigo, Duke of Urbino. Imbued with all the enthusiasm of the age for the new learning and the arts, he spent all his spare cash and energy on the construction and embellishment of the Tempio, assembling the best artists of the time, in the face of continual difficulties. His vicious moral character has probably been largely exaggerated, owing partly to the personal animosity of Aeneas Silvius Piccolomini (Pius II) and partly to the propaganda of the Church that was out to despoil him of his possessions. An heroic and pathetic figure, always fighting a losing

battle against fate, he died with nearly all his territories lost to him, and a half-finished edifice—that remains, nevertheless, the most eloquent monument of its epoch.

That Sigismondo "was the most representative personality of his time" is doubtful, but to Pound he is by far the most admirable. As a *condottieri* of the Quattrocento, he was involved in the most complicated political maneuvers; and his lifelong struggle to enlarge his own domain or even to unify the realm that was historically the property of the Malatesta family met with continual reverses. He was one of the petty tyrants of his day, and his importance as a moving force in Italian politics was, like that of others of his class, secondary to the importance of such powers as Milan, Florence, Venice, Naples, the Pope, and the Medici banking empire. In spite of his courage, energy, and shrewdness, Sigismondo was unable to avoid being used by these powers for their own purposes. Throughout his life he was engaged by one or another of them to lead their armies, and he shifted his allegiances as easily as they shifted their alliances. Always fighting, hardly ever out of danger, constantly betrayed by a change of policy at a higher level, he continued to struggle, with whatever means he had at his disposal, for the integration of the kingdom he considered to be his.

Like other men of his class and time, he was suspected, and perhaps guilty, of outrageous crimes. It was said that he had attempted to rape a German pilgrim to Rome on her way home from Church; when she resisted, he killed her and raped her corpse. A wife whom he had contracted as a matter of policy died mysteriously, reportedly by poison; another wife met a similar strange death; and Sigismondo fathered his children on other women, notably on Isotta degli Atti, a lady of Rimini, who became at last his third wife. It is to the love of Isotta and Sigismondo that the Tempio is said to be a monument.

Between his military and sexual encounters Sigismondo managed to find time for the Tempio, and it is the construction of this masterwork which, for Pound, most strongly distinguishes Sigismondo from his scheming contemporaries. The letters quoted in the Malatesta Cantos give evidence of Sigismondo's concern with the Tempio's artistic excellence, and of his respect for art and artists. These Cantos likewise record his veneration for Gemisto Plethon, the Byzantine philosopher whose visit to Italy in 1438–1440 stimulated interest in classical literature and philosophy. When Gemisto died a few years later, Sigismondo had his ashes interred in the Tempio in one of the many places of honor reserved therein for such distinguished men.

For the building of the Tempio Sigismondo

> secured the services of some of the most distinguished artists and craftsmen of his time—Leon Battista Alberti, Matteo da Pasti, Simone Ferucci, Agostino di Duccio, and others.[6]

The others include Piero della Francesca, Pisanello, and Giovanni Bellini. As the letter at the beginning of Canto VIII indicates, Sigismondo believed in treating his craftsmen well, recognizing the artist's need to work in his own way. The building itself has been described as follows:

> Reconstructed on the framework of the 13th century Gothic church of San Francesco at Rimini, the Tempio is an impressive monument of early Renaissance style, and one of the boldest and most splendid achievements of the period. Begun in 1446, it was consecrated in 1450. Work was interrupted in 1455, leaving the façade and transept uncompleted, and the dome not even begun.[7]

Pound's admiration of Sigismondo and his great work is extreme:

> If you consider the Malatesta and Sigismondo in particular, a failure, he was at all events a failure worth all the successes of his age. He had in Rimini,

> Pisanello, Pier della Francesca. Rimini still has 'the best Bellini in Italy.' If the Tempio is a jumble and junk shop, it nevertheless registers a concept. There is no other single man's effort equally registered. [*GK*, Frontispiece]

And again:

> The Tempio Malatestiano is both an apex and in verbal sense a monumental failure. It is perhaps the apex of what one man has embodied in the last 1000 years of the occident. A cultural 'high' is marked.
>
> In a Europe not YET rotted by usury, but outside the then system, and pretty much against the power that was, and in any case without great material resources, Sigismondo cut his notch. He registered a state of mind, of sensibility, of all-roundedness and awareness. [*GK*, 159]

Later in the same passage Pound writes: "All that a single man could, Malatesta managed *against* the current of power."

For the presentation of such a figure as Malatesta, Pound is faced with a double problem. He must register the sensibility of Malatesta as it existed against the background of fifteenth-century Italy, and he must indicate the relevance of this material to the modern world. In effect, what he must do is show both the historicity and the contemporaneity of the situation of Malatesta. Through quotations, translations, and paraphrases of fifteenth-century letters, pronouncements, narratives, poems, and inscriptions, Pound presents the world in which Sigismondo lived, even to the extent of identifying himself with Sigismondo's partisans:

> And the Angevins were gunning after Naples
> And we dragged in the Angevins,
> And we dragged in Louis Eleventh,
> And the *tiers Calixte* was dead, and Alfonso; Alfonse le roi, etc.

And against us we had 'this Æeneas' and young
Ferdinando
That we had smashed at Piombino and driven out
of the
Terrene of the Florentines. . . . [Canto X]

This is the technique of the mask, and it is used not only to associate Pound and the speaker in a common sympathy with Malatesta, but also as an objective correlative of the modern poet's sense of Malatesta's world. At the same time Pound introduces into the account modern colloquialisms that suggest—what the persona cannot know—that the techniques used by Sigismondo's enemies to defraud him are not altogether unknown today:

'that Messire Alessandro Sforza
is become lord of Pèsaro
through the wangle of the Illus. Sgr. Mr. Fedricho
d'Orbino
Who worked the wangle with Galeaz
through the wiggling of Messer Francesco,
Who waggled it so that Galeaz should sell Pèsaro
to Alex and Fossembrone to Feddy. . . .'
[Canto IX]

Through these devices the events of fifteenth-century Italy are presented both as a record of the achievement of one man at a difficult time and as a touchstone of human achievement for any time. All the writing of Pound is concerned with the working out of decent values in a world that is usually antagonistic to decent values. Among those who have managed it Malatesta is a brilliant example. John Adams is another, Pietro Leopoldo a third; and other Cantos present still other men who are heroes by this standard.

As, in his "translations" of Propertius, Pound associated himself with the emotions of his subject and found those emotions to be as appropriate in 1917 as they had been in Propertius' time, so in *The Cantos* Pound associates himself with the general situation and purpose which are common to the heroes of his long poem. Like them he has certain values and is involved in a lifelong struggle to affirm those values; against the enmity of connivers everywhere he and a few friends, like Malatesta and *his* few friends, try to "cut their notch," to "register a state of mind, of sensibility, of all-roundedness and awareness." So he says of Malatesta's astuteness in getting the finest artists of his age to work at the Tempio:

> He had a little of the best there in Rimini. He had perhaps Zuan Bellin's best bit of painting. He had all he cd. get of Pier della Francesca. Federigo Urbino was his Amy Lowell, Federigo with more wealth got the seconds. [*GK*, 159]

Malatesta was to "Feddy" what Pound is to Amy. While Pound encouraged Yeats, Eliot, Joyce, Gaudier-Brzeska, and Wyndham Lewis, Amy "with more wealth" fussed at the corpse of Imagism.

But while Pound associates his own modern position with the positions of Malatesta and other heroes of *The Cantos*, he actually presents these heroes less from the inside than from the outside. His speakers are as often admirers of his heroes as the heroes themselves. But he gives to the speakers and the events they record a contemporary idiom and a contemporary application. The struggle is the same in any age, and the addition of contemporaneity to an old speech is necessary to the purpose of *The Cantos*. The purpose is to make a poem that will be to the reader as well as the writer a correlative of the modern world. And, consequently, the situations presented are not of importance to the personae; the personae are important to the situations. The personae do not change, do not develop, do not undergo significant experiences; their experiences tell them only what they already know, or at best bring home the irony of their situations a little more pointedly. Pound is almost alone among modern poets in his refusal to treat internal histories in his poems. His personae stolidly remain what they are from the beginning—which, as it partially illuminates Pound's indifference to the theatre, also tends to make the states of consciousness, of which his poems are correlatives, more "objective" as Pound would call it, more "lifeless" as T. E. Hulme might admiringly confess, or, as Gaudier-Brzeska would put it, more "monumental."

And this is true of Pound himself as he appears in *The Cantos.* He appears frequently, recalling people he has known and the words they have spoken and all that he has seen and done. But he does not change. *The Cantos* rotates around him as its stable center, around Pound as the mature observer, pulling together all the pieces of his pattern. As the Cantos proceed, the echoes accumulate until in the Pisan Cantos the "I" of the poem has become a series of memories; from itself as center it recapitulates the substance of all that has gone before and reaffirms the central values to which the poem itself is, like Malatesta's Tempio, a monument. The "I" itself, drawing heavily on the historical facts of Pound's career, is nevertheless a technique of perspective (and texture) subordinate to the fundamental matter of the poem: the affirmation of the value of intelligent action.

As the early mask was a superimposition of a modern awareness on ancient or near-ancient awareness, so the "I" of *The Cantos* represents that modern awareness embedded in modern actuality. The subject of Pound's poem is the modern world and its relation to permanent human values, particularly as this relation is manifested in the recurrent struggle of gifted individuals against the corruption of their contemporaries. In the presentation the modern "I" finds his own struggle echoed in the intelligent action of Malatesta, Confucius, John Adams, Odysseus, and others. But the "I" remains central, the continuing voice of Pound, the projection of Pound into the poem, witness to all past glory and to all present degeneration, living in all the worlds at once—in old Greece, old China, old Provence and Italy, and also in modern America and England, climates in which everything, like Eleanor of Aquitaine, has "spoiled" (Canto VII) or almost everything, for there are still a few valuable individuals who keep on struggling against the furious stupidity of the world. Much like Tiresias in *The Waste Land*, the persona in *The Cantos* serves as a point of fusion for all the characters in the poem, and not only for the characters but for the scenes and civilizations as well. The meeting place of the past and the present is the consciousness that is aware of both of them, a consciousness that deepens the past by providing for it the new context of the present, and deepens the present by insisting on its connection, its thematic connection, with what has gone before. In *The Cantos,* as in *The Waste Land,* all has been "foresuffered," and it is fitting that the poem begins with the actual figure of Tiresias, up from Hell, prophesying to Odysseus the terrible journey before him, the journey that, as *The Cantos* shows us in detail (and as Pound's life ironically bears out), lies before any man of imagination in a hostile world. For it is a world in which both imagination and hostility to it are recurrent, and in which not only the conflict between them, but the achievement drawn out of the conflict, are permanent:

> 'Odysseus
> 'Shalt return through spiteful Neptune, over dark
> seas,
> 'Lose all companions.'

This "I" is an objectification, in the form of the person of Pound himself, of that superior consciousness that had always inhabited the mask poems and still speaks through the modern colloquialisms of old personae. But it now speaks not only through Pound and his other personae, but also through the poem, through the whole of *The Cantos*. The experiencer turns over the leaves of his memory and sets down, apparently at random, his intellectual experiences along with the passion they engender. But what he sets down is, piece by piece, of uncertain importance. Only when the memory grows extensive enough to include virtually the whole modern world do we fully see that *The Cantos* is not merely a personal outburst but a recording of the experience of civilization. And we see, too, that the "I" is a spokesman for that superior consciousness that the reader is invited to share. The whole poem (or as much of it as we have) presents the *feel* of the modern world through a necessary feeling subject. Not that subject but the world, is the matter of the poem. The "I" is its presenter, its singer; the poem is his song, his monument. Yet even while the persona wanders among his memories, we feel the presence of a still fuller intelligence superintending the wandering. We feel the poet in his poem as the singing persona, but we also feel him behind the poem's pattern as the composer of this enormous song. There is point in all the random memories, order in all the apparent meandering. The poem is not really a song written line by line and Canto by Canto; it is a song already unified by the *virtu* of its creator, a song that only needs to be put in "verbal manifestation" in order to *be* a song (although of course therein lies the whole story). The "I" serves as immediate perspective on all the events recorded, but the fuller, and necessary, perspective can be grasped only as we meet the superior awareness of the artist in our assimilation of the poem's structure—indeed, of the poem's feel. To find the poem as an experience, we must ultimately abandon our identification with the persona and share the perspective of the consciousness that has made the poem.

5

Conclusion

In the foregoing survey of Eliot, Yeats, and Pound I have tried to show that these poets characteristically detach themselves from their personae and invite the reader to share with the poet a fuller consciousness of the poem. They expect the reader rather to undergo the poem as an experience than to accompany the persona through his experiences. The personae serve as instances, not as exemplars; yet the ultimate hero of such modern poems is, in a way, still the poet himself, who is felt, through all the poetic elements including the persona, as the definitive force within the poem. However intent he is on his presentation of reality, what he presents is ultimately not reality but a "vision" of it, a "statement" of it, a "replacement" of it, which is pervaded with the "colour," the "tone," the "*virtu*," of the poet. The poetry of these men is as "personal" as any poetry.

Yet the way in which it is personal is different from most nineteenth-century verse, and its difference rests in its abandonment of the persona as the center of the poem (and, implicitly, of the world). But as soon as the persona ceases to be central in a poem which he speaks and which purports to present his own experiences (as even the unobtrusive "I" of a novel or narrative poem shares his point of view, and hence his own experience, with the reader), the lyric situation clearly becomes a mask for something more subtle. Even Browning resembles his nineteenth-century contemporaries in using his poetry to present person after person; the era sometimes seems an endless (and fascinating) parade of people, experience piled on experience, life piled on life. The three poets whose work has been the subject of this study do not present people as people. They present situations inhabited by people. For their poems attempt to give the reader a sense of the structure of human reality; and however oblique the scheme of presentation, people must be part of that scheme, if only as the implicit speakers of the words of this verbal art.

Furthermore, even the schematizations of reality which these poets choose as the subject of their poetry have no validity unless the reader verifies their validity in his own consciousness. The structure of the world, for which the form of the poem serves as trope, is, insofar as it is ever formulated in abstract language, itself an abstract linguistic symbol for patterns of feeling. The poet's feeling orders itself doubly—in the rational formulations about the nature of the universe which we detect in the poem, and in the affective formulation of the poem, which makes use of the rational formulations. Ultimately, the poet's consciousness communicates with the reader's consciousness, and proposes through the poem a nondiscursive, even nonlinguistic definition of an area of common feeling.

Poet talks to reader about what they relate to similarly—the peculiar system of responses which defines the human animal and governs his assimilation of everything outside him. But although the system is basically the same in poet and reader, patterns of emotional response differ from person to person as widely as fingerprints and faces. Every poet, whatever his manner or his school, takes for his province a range and depth of feeling idiosyncratic to him. He thus gives to the common subject of all poets a shape and density that mark his work as individual. In the forging of this individuality, the choice of genre, method, surface subject, kinds of personae, structural techniques, and formulated beliefs, guided as each choice is by the usages of the past, all function as symbolically significant contributions to the poet's variation on the elemental human communication. To "respond" to a poem is to verify the assertion of the poet that human feeling, whatever else it may be (and it is so many things at once that poets can never exhaust it), is also *this*.

The poets treated here indicate both through their practice and through their criticism that they hold some such view of the nature of poetry—of all poetry, not only their own. And they judge a poet according to how successfully he has put together tones and textures and structures symbolic of human feeling. Largely through their influence modern critics have come to regard personae and the events that take place on the surface of poems, even of Romantic poems, as less significant than the implications of their formal properties. To put it another way, modern critics have difficulty projecting themselves into Romantic personae and tend to read Romantic poems as masks rather than as confessional reports. We feel today that, whatever "sincere" poets think they do or are credited with doing, any power derived from their poetry is due to their largely unconscious approximations of complex emotional patterns, approximations effected through the mask of particular experiences. In a way, the poetic theory to which a poet subscribes matters little to our final evaluation of him; so long as he remains true to the fundamental feeling-structure within him and sensitive to the contemporary world as a *medium* for conveying that feeling-structure, his rational formulations are of small consequence. The Romantic poet, in spite of himself, writes a poem that is a mask.

But even if such a theory sounds valid, we still have no satisfactory critical machinery for demonstrating how combinations of poetic elements succeed in being felt as significant of patterns of feeling. Although modern criticism may seem to have penetrated into some of the psychology of poem-making and poem-reading, we still tend, along with critics of other ages, to expend our industry rather on the mask than on how the mask reveals what it does reveal. We have a habit of thinking that we explain a poem when we analyze the intellectual techniques employed by the poet, but even when we go so far as to try to explain the intellectual effect, we rarely go further to show what content of human feeling the intellectual effect possesses. Like earlier critics, or even unsophisticated contemporaries, who think they have done enough when they show a poem to be "sincere," or "passionate," we customarily think we have done enough when we show a poem to be "subtle," or "complex." Perhaps our criticism needs, more than anything else, a sense of the due importance of historical ideas to the *mask*, along with a sense of the ultimate unimportance of any ideas to the *poem*.

For although cultural changes in poetic theory enhance some reputations and depress others, the best poets can usually be justified by any theory, and it often appears that the good critic is he who can grasp the virtues of any poet, can feel his way through the conventional, era-given characteristics to the patterns of feeling which a poem shadows forth. Thus, Shakespeare and Wordsworth write lyrics in sharply different ways: Shakespeare's persona is a singer, Wordsworth's is a professional man, a poet; Shakespeare relies on the reader to see the artificial qualities of his verse, Wordsworth tries to reduce the role of illusion in his work to a minimum; Shakespeare's achievement is his song, Wordsworth's his imagination. But though their approaches differ in a thousand details, the poems of both serve as communications of feeling objectified in a verbal form. All the events, pronouncements, and personae ultimately function in a form that masks—that is, asserts and concentrates, not hides—the peculiar patterns of feeling which distinguish the poet.

What, then, is the significance of the historical changes in the uses of personae? Simply: we must understand the mask in order to understand, to feel accurately, what it reveals. And since the mask that any poem is, composes its features out of contemporary moral and intellectual systems, out of the biographical limitations of the poet, out of the economic and social and poetic traditions of his age, out of all, in fact, that we study as relevant to a poem, only a proper sense of all these ingredients as they figure in the mask will enable us to grasp most comprehensively what lies beneath the mask. Criticism helps us to assess justly the poem's overt relation to its moment of composition; for it is merely this relation that comprises the mask. And although the critic must at some point not only stand aside from his sympathy with the persona, he must also accept only partially the invitation of the poet to share in the experience of the poem as a first- or second-person activity; the final labor of criticism is to detach oneself from all identification, and, using one's knowledge of what such identification may be and is in this particular case, to evaluate almost as a third person, with all the information one has and all the breadth of understanding one can efficiently tolerate, the success with which the poet reveals, through the poem as mask, feeling at its most significant.

For the achievement of this aim the study of personae can be a most instructive tool. The brief history sketched in chapter 1 attempts only to survey the subject and to suggest lines of development for future students of personae. Although we customarily refer to the speaker in our definition of genres, we seldom look at him full face and see him as what he in fact is, the center of our own definitions. Problems of poetic kinds could well be illuminated by a comparative study of the speakers traditionally considered appropriate to each. Modern critics have already begun to examine the content of satiric personae, but the study has scarcely tested its wings. We need to recognize the great importance of the "I" to any poem—to any mask—and to see that the ambiguity inherent in the word is the starting point not only of satire and irony, modes that obviously rely on the reader's perception of the speaker's multiplicity, but also of *all* fiction if not, indeed, of all writing whatsoever. Another study, suggested at almost every point of this work, is of the relation between the dramatic monologue and satire, two forms with apparently different purposes and effects but with strikingly similar structures. Finally, contemporary criticism requires a fuller understanding of the poet's sense, largely objectified in conventions, of his audience, a deeper awareness of the uses, and their import, to which a poet may put the conventional expectations of his readers.

It remains to say something final about Eliot, Yeats, and Pound. Whether one regards these poets as classic or romantic, or fixes their work in other more or less meaningful categories than these, it seems clear that personae and other surface elements of their poetry are of an importance subordinate to that of the poem taken as a whole, and taken as a whole experience, an experience of human reality. Thus the subjective orientation of a persona-centered poetry gives way to a totality-oriented poetry in which the world and the poet's sense of it, its objective structure and its feel, are scarcely to be distinguished. Self and world, persona and his surroundings, poet and his poem, are tightly bound to each other, their interaction and their mutual responsibilities permanent objective features of human actuality, discontinuously existing each in its defining counterpart.

To be sure, personae are always subordinate to poems, always instrumental to the meanings that poems are and participate in—as instrumental, indeed, in their fitting the structure of poems with coherent perspectives as are the very words themselves through which sound is brought to form and hence to meaning. In this all poems are similar. But words without meanings have no value, and all intellectual meanings are products of conventional agreement. Poems can hence be understood only in terms of the conventional agreements that validate, if only for a time, their verbal patterns. Why they are so validated, why some patterns and not others can be accepted as proper for reader to expect and for poet to provide, is the deep aesthetic question. But the verbal pattern of a poem, conceived in relation to what for its time is the acceptable range of validated verbal patterns, comprises the poem's mask. And while personae are always subordinate to poems, they are often central in the mask. For Eliot, for Yeats, and for Pound personae serve to locate perspectives, but in the structures of thought and sound which comprise the mask the personae yield their central position to the self-and-world situation that for these three poets defines reality.

Notes

CHAPTER 1.

[1] Adolf Trendelenburg, "A Contribution to the History of the Word Person: A Posthumous Treatise," tr. Carl H. Haessler, *The Monist*, XX, 1 (Jan., 1910), 349. Much of the speculation of the next few pages is based on evidence supplied by Trendelenburg's essay.

[2] *Ibid.*, p. 346.

[3] That these and virtually all human activities can be interpreted as developments of play, as J. Huizinga suggests in *Homo Ludens* (Boston, 1950), or as symbolic activities, as Ernst Cassirer argues in *An Essay on Man* (Garden City, N. Y., 1953) and elsewhere, only confirms these assertions. For play itself may be interpreted as a universally human symbolic activity, and all such activities seem to be formalizations of common human impulses, and ultimately of that impulse toward symbolization itself through which alone the dialogue can *become* talk.

[4] Trendelenburg, *op. cit.*, p. 353.

[5] *Ibid.*, p. 347.

[6] *Ibid.*, p. 353.

[7] Or, in Jung's different terminology, the conscious, the personal unconscious, and the racial unconscious. Examples could be multiplied from other fields. In most sports and games, for instance, there is a competitor, his antagonist, and an umpire or rules that serve as an objective referent, a persona who represents the conditions under which the competition takes place, conditions that include, as in the courtroom, objective judgment between the two parties.

[8] *A History of Literary Criticism in the Renaissance* (New York, 1899), pp. 58–59.

[9] *An Introduction to Poetry* (New York, 1909), p. 55.

[10] The best direct theoretical discussions of personae appear in William B. Ewald's *The Masks of Jonathan Swift* (Cambridge, Mass., 1954), Rebecca Price Parkin's *The Poetic Workmanship of Alexander Pope* (Minneapolis, 1955), and Maynard Mack's "The Muse of Satire," *Yale Review*, XLI (Autumn, 1951), 80–92. Hugh Kenner's *The Poetry of Ezra Pound* (London, 1951) and H. H. Watts's *Ezra*

Pound and the Cantos (London, 1951) include studies of Pound's personae; Warren Ramsey's *Jules Laforgue and the Ironic Inheritance* (New York, 1953) studies Laforgue's "voices"; Richard Ellmann's *Yeats: The Man and the Masks* (New York, 1948) and *The Identity of Yeats* (New York, 1954) examine Yeats's multiple poses and their implications. These, along with Robert Langbaum's *The Poetry of Experience* (New York, 1957), which bears on the subject at every point, are valuable to any student of personae.

[11] From *The Beautiful Changes and Other Poems,* copyright, 1947, by Richard Wilbur. Reprinted by permission of Harcourt, Brace and Company, Inc.

[12] Such a division is, of course, common and almost inevitable wherever the lyric tradition is oral.

[13] See, for a perceptive treatment of this problem, Robert Langbaum's *The Poetry of Experience* (New York, 1957), especially "Introduction: Romanticism as a Modern Tradition."

[14] *Ibid.*, p. 94.

[15] From *Selected Poems* by Richard Eberhart. 1951. Reprinted by permission of Oxford University Press, Inc.

Chapter 2.

[1] In his 1931 essay, "Charles Whibley," Eliot notes that "there are only four ways of thinking: to talk to others, or to one other, or to talk to oneself, or to talk to God." [*SE*, 447] By 1953 Eliot had come to limit the number to *The Three Voices of Poetry,* but *Four Quartets* may use these four voices without clearly discriminating among them. In a way, the poem is addressed to all four audiences at once, so that the four voices "melt" into one another, like "music heard so deeply / That it is not heard at all, but you are the music / While the music lasts."

Chapter 3.

[1] *Per Amica Silentia Lunae* (New York, 1918), pp. 21–23. Cf. *Auto,* p. 208.

Chapter 4.

[1] *Sewanee Review,* LIII, 2, 3, 4 (Spring, Summer, Autumn, 1945).

[2] All of Pound's poems except *The Cantos* are quoted in this chapter from *Personae: Collected Shorter Poems of Ezra Pound* (London, 1952). Copyright 1926 by Ezra Pound. Reprinted by permission of New Directions. The bracketed figures refer to the page numbers of this volume. Excerpts from *The Cantos* are quoted from *The Cantos of Ezra Pound* (New York, 1948). Copyright 1934, 1937, 1940, 1948 by Ezra Pound. Reprinted by permission of New Directions.

[3] In "Further Notes on Mauberley," *Accent,* XVI, 1 (Winter, 1956), 59–67.

[4] *Ezra Pound's Mauberley* (Berkeley and Los Angeles, 1955), p. 3.

[5] Ed. Peter Russell (Norfolk, Conn., n.d.), p. 106. All rights reserved. Reprinted by permission of New Directions.

[6] Robert Mayo, "A Guide to Canto VIII," *Analyst* (Dept. of English, Northwestern University), V (Oct., 1954), 6.

[7] *Ibid.*

The Poet in the Poem

Every lyric poem is an instance of dramatic speech, and requires the reader to distinguish between the poet and his persona, or speaker. Yet between these two there is in every poem an implicit sensibility that somehow inhabits the whole poetic structure and may be taken to be the poet in the poem.

The divergence between the point of view of the personae and the point of view of the poets is what gives much of modern poetry its impersonal quality, its ambiguity, its indirection, its ironic, oblique manner of statement. But this use of personae, though more deliberately conscious and marked in our time, is not altogether new.

This volume, which focuses on Eliot, Yeats, and Pound, is the first to study personae as a structural element of all poems. Although most writers see personae as a means for obscuring the poet's real self, Wright sees them as a device for asserting what explicit self-expression is incapable of asserting. He elaborates the various and individual uses these three poets have made of personae, and the manner in which they have thus been able to image their world in terms that would not have been possible through explicit statement. The analysis is both clarifying and enlightening, and results in a deepened understanding of that world and of what a poem is.

GEORGE T. WRIGHT is Associate Professor of English at the University of Tennessee.

UNIVERSITY OF CALIFORNIA PRESS
Address: Berkeley 4, California